WEDDING PLANNING SUCKS

WEDDING PLANNING *Sucks*

HOW TO CONQUER THE PROCESS WITH LESS STRESS

R.J. HUPCHER

OPEN BAR
PUBLISHING

NEW YORK

Copyright © 2021 by Robert Hupcher

All rights reserved. No part of this book may be reproduced or used in any manner without written permission of the copyright owner except for the use of quotations in a book review.

Limit of Liability: Although the publisher and the author have made every effort to ensure that the information in this book was correct at press time and while this work is designed to provide accurate information in regard to the subject matter covered, the publisher and the author assume no responsibility for errors, inaccuracies, omissions, or any other inconsistencies herein and hereby disclaim any liability to any party for any loss, damage, or disruption caused by errors or omissions, whether such errors or omissions result from negligence, accident, or any other cause. Readers should be aware that Internet websites listed in this work may have changed or disappeared between when this work was written and when it is read.

This work is sold with the understanding that neither the publisher nor the author is engaged in rendering medical, legal, financial, or professional advice. This work is meant as a source of valuable information for the reader, however it is not meant as a substitute for direct expert assistance. If such level of assistance is required, the services of a competent professional should be sought.

Published in the United States by Open Bar Publishing

ISBN 978-0-578-93092-3 (paperback)
ISBN 978-0-578-93093-0 (e-book)

Library of Congress Control Number: 2021912294

Editor: Bodie Dykstra
Interior Designer: Phillip Gessert
Indexer: Shirley Agen

Cover Designer: Danielle Camorlinga
Graphic Designer: Wayne Woon
Glass Designers: Seren Skye and IselArt Design
Interior Textbox Images: © Alexander Lysenko, © Islam Islamzada,
© ARCHWIN-AKIRA, © solomon7/shutterstock.com

www.weddingplanningsucks.com

*For Jen, the absolute love of my life.
Without you, there would be no wedding to write about.*

TABLE OF CONTENTS

SO WE BEGIN... 1
Introduction 1
Who the heck do I think I am? 3
What to expect from this book 5

I. GETTING STARTED 11
Communication 13
You can have your say in this thing (if you want to) 16
Priorities, expectations, compromises, and other fun words 17
The bride is always right (?) 25
Staying organized 27
Wedding planners (not you, the professionals) 32

II. BUDGETING, YOUR LIFEJACKET 37
Your personal financial situation 40
How much wedding can I afford? 42
Budgeting apps, a life-changing experience 47
Safekeeping with the FDIC 49
Breaking down costs 52
Putting your spreadsheet to work 59
The perfect budget and other fairy tales 61

III. KEEPING STRESS IN CHECK 65
Eustress vs. distress 68
Tackling your to-do list, one layer of snow at a time 70
"Just think positively," they said 72
It (only) takes two to tango 74
SOS and asking for help 77
Catharsis 79
Never forget the why 82
Your life does not stop for wedding planning 83
Things will go wrong 87

In conclusion, bad stress bad..91

IV. INTERMISSION 93

V. A TIME AND A PLACE..97
Let's date..99
Location, location, location 101
On-site vs. off-site catering..104
House of worship vs. on-site ceremony..107
All the (venue) questions 109
Contracts and costs..117
Negotiating and not losing your shi(r)t...119
Hotels..122

VI. VENDORS AND FEEDING FRENZIES 125
Photography and paparazzi (part I)...127
Yes, they are just flowers...135
Beats..140
Eat it..149
Making it official...157

VII. TO YOUR HEAD COUNT, FROM YOUR GUESTS..163
Save-the-dates..165
Guest count: guests count...167
Invitations..169
Navigating the wedding registry..174

VIII. ODDS AND ENDS...177
Odds: decorations, DIY, and random additions 179
Ends: honeymooning..184

IX. IT'S THE FINAL COUNTDOWN....................................187
Vows..189
Photography and paparazzi (part II, finally) 191
Wedding-day tips...194
Deliverance: into the sunset...197

AFTERWORD 199
WORKS CITED 201
INDEX 203

SO WE BEGIN...

INTRODUCTION

Hi there. Looks like you have a wedding coming up. Lucky you. I did that once. At the beginning of my wedding-planning escapade, I would have given you a pat on the back and chuckled a hearty "good luck" as I fled. That's because when I started my wedding journey, I was in a terrible place, paralyzed by stress.

Amid the process, however, I grew as a person. If I had to do it again (please, God, no), I'm confident I would weather the storm much more effectively. I changed my mindset and learned ways to cope with and even harness wedding-planning stress. In short, I'm here to teach you everything I learned so you have an easier time.

Look, everyone needs their hand held for *something*—perhaps for learning how to ride a bike or finding that elusive first job. For me, as I'm not ashamed to admit, it was wedding planning. I was like a young fan desperately reaching out to high-five a superstar, but my outstretched hand was left hanging, and I stumbled through the marathon without suitable guidance.

With the prevalence of wedding resources, you're probably skeptical about that statement. I would be, too. After all, the wedding industry is an absolute behemoth that generates $70 billion per year. Surely, there must have been *something*—a book, a blog, a magazine, a podcast—to guide me down the Yellow Brick Road.

Take a closer look at my statement. I said "suitable" guidance. Before you roll your eyes, please allow me to explain. I think you may find my defense compelling.

I started doing wedding-planning research once I begrudgingly accepted that I would have to count wedding planning as a life experience. It was overwhelming and unrelatable. There were blogs about cheerful brides, books about being frugal to the point of being cheap, and entire websites devoted to creating "your perfect day." Some resources hit closer to the mark, but precisely zero focused on what I needed: a way for a stressed-out realist to plan a wedding without experiencing (too much) misery along the way.

By its very nature, wedding planning is a stressful affair. Most sane people accept this or at least expect a few stumbling blocks. I, a fellow sane person, was expecting the stress as well. However, there's a massive difference between expecting something and being prepared for it. Because I wasn't prepared for the stress, I languished in it. It's fair to say I hated wedding planning. Hence the book title.

The stress led to a slew of feelings, none of them positive—guilt, stress, animosity, and resentment, to name a few. I needed a resource to help pull me out of this spiral, but I found none. Surely there were others like me who were not particularly optimistic about the challenges ahead.

As you could imagine, it became awkward when family and friends mentioned wedding planning—usually with a grin and a laugh—and assumed I was rapturous to be arranging that "special day." My parents were giddy; her folks were ecstatic. It seemed like everyone wanted my fiancé and me to have a wedding except for, well, me. My perspective *at the time* was that weddings were a colossal waste of time and money.

This obviously strained my relationship with my fiancé. Although her stress ebbed and flowed, her attitude was generally more positive than mine, and that kept me from walking off the proverbial ledge. In fact, I'm not sure I would have pulled through without her.

So why introduce this? Simple: to show you where I began. Spoiler alert, *my wedding ended up being one of the best days of my life.* I never imagined looking back on my wedding with such fondness. If you're holding this book, you've obviously found yourself confronted with the daunting prospect of organizing a wedding. You recognize it will be stressful and you're seeking a means to endure the process. You've opened the right book.

Even if you're oozing positivity about wedding planning, this book is for you—so long as you're interested in reducing your stress along the way.

This book will help pull you into the proper wedding-planning mindset, and adopting that mindset makes *all* the difference.

You're probably wondering about the "suitable" advice I was putting forth before. It's quite simple and—no surprise here—it's in the title. I'm hoping to bestow upon you the advice I was sorely missing and show you how to make it through the process with less stress. You don't want stress to torture you, especially during the multi-month endeavor that is wedding planning. No one does. I have your back. If a poor soul like me can survive this and grow along the way, so can you. My job is to prove it to you.

Speaking of my job...

WHO THE HECK DO I THINK I AM?

Even though I hate this part, I think it's necessary to offer you some insight into my frame of reference. I would write this book anonymously if I didn't consider it entirely creepy to have an anonymous author write about weddings. Maybe I'll employ a fun pen name for when I compose the sequel, *Divorces Suck: How to Conquer the Process with More Assets*, by R.J. Hunter. Just kidding, baby. Please don't drag me to Zumba again.

So, I'm Rob and I started this book when I was 30 years old. Only time will tell how old I'll be when I finish it. I live in a small New York City apartment with my lovely wife, Jen, and our two cats, Dex and Lena. Our apartment is old and has thin walls. In fact, sometimes our neighbor, Waleed, gets amped up for no apparent reason and we can hear him yelling and clapping and laughing (all at the same time), so I also consider Waleed a member of our household. We're hoping to move soon. Waleed will stay here.

I investigate financial crimes—but don't *commit* financial crimes—which is why so much of my wedding stress stemmed from money. Jen is a speech-language pathologist and mostly teaches children, so she is well-equipped to reason with me.

Jen and I met in college and dated for about 10 years before we got married. She hated me when she first got to know me, and I assume her sentiment has only marginally improved since then. She likes to remind me of that all the time, especially when people comment on how long we were together prior to getting married.

We were engaged for about 18 months before tying the knot. If you thought that was a lengthy engagement, you would be right. This was mainly because we needed time to save money. It was also a result of preferring not to wed during New York's unbearably humid summer. After considering some cost constraints, we ultimately settled on a November wedding. Fear not—in the venue section, we'll explore an abundance of points you should examine when choosing a site and date. It's not overly complicated.

We picked a venue that enabled us to have the ceremony, cocktail hour, and reception all in one locale. A hotel was attached to the venue, so most revelers could safely stumble back to their rooms at night's end without concerns about driving—an added bonus. We had around 160 guests with a healthy mix of locals and out-of-towners. In case it's not painfully obvious, we planned our own wedding.

As I set forth before, I do *not* work in the wedding industry. I had a wedding, I did considerable research along the way, and I've attended weddings. Those are my only qualifications. I don't even love weddings. Ironic, huh?

I *am*, however, a maestro in wedding stress, extensively trained by experience. I understand the immense stress firsthand, not secondhand through what my clients advise me. On that point, I'm not searching for business from you, I'm not seeking to sign you up for anything, and I'm certainly not looking for clients. I don't have a wedding business, remember? This is a standalone book with some free additional content on my website. You have a copy, so you've managed your part. Now it's time for me to do mine, which is to supply you with the knowledge to wildly improve your wedding-planning experience.

LET'S TALK WEDDINGS

Since I've thrown a bunch of shade at weddings, you deserve to understand why. I don't suspect these to be earth-shattering revelations because, well, I'm not an earth-shattering person. The cardinal grievance I have with weddings is the cost. Weddings are stupidly expensive, and sadly, you will be quoted ridiculous amounts of money for the simplest of additions.

Second, a wedding adds, in my own humble opinion, unnecessary stress on everybody involved in designing it, from the future bride and groom to their parents, friends, siblings, colleagues, and probably even pets, although I am still completing my scientific study to confirm. They are stressful for *everyone.*

Third, even though your pictures will endure forever, the wedding itself only lasts one night. So much sweat and money are riding on that one night, and all it takes is one mishap to potentially taint all your preparations (note my second point).

Last, no matter how much money, effort, sweat, and attention to detail you invest, it's expected that at least some guests will be critical of the wedding. They'll be sure to broadcast these judgments.

Phew—that was a lot. Just in case you missed it the first time, it's worth noting again: these *were* my views during wedding planning. My attitude became more optimistic as I worked through the process and discovered how to combat each of my above grievances. You'll learn how to do this, too, of course. My wedding experience was spectacular. I demand the same spectacular experience for you but *without* the mental anguish. That's the entire purpose of this book.

I wager that some of what I said resonates with you. In fact, I think it's all an honest look. However, I won't be offended if you find that ridiculous, stop reading here, curse me for the time you just squandered, and go do something more productive, like—oh, I don't know—stress about your wedding.

If you're still with me, let's peek behind the curtain to explore how we're going to transform your wedding journey from scaling Mount Everest to waddling up an icy driveway. Still treacherous, but far less likely to kill you.

WHAT TO EXPECT FROM THIS BOOK

At some point after meeting the beautiful woman who is now my wife, I advised her to manage her expectations of me. This way she wouldn't be disappointed, and I'd have infinite chances to impress her with my adulting skills, like making eggs and taking showers. It was a win-win, and I credit that (and ice cream) for our relationship success.

Based on that segue, you're probably thinking you should manage your expectations of this book as well. Quite the contrary, this book is objectively more impressive than my dilapidated omelets. However, I still want to be direct with you. You deserve clarity about what you're signing up for. Anything less is disrespectful to you *and* your time.

So here's a brief rundown of what's to follow.

Part I—Getting started. When Jimi Hendrix strummed his first guitar, he was terrible (probably). However, he had to start *somewhere*. It's the same for wedding planning. This section starts you off on the right foot with the process, with your partner, and with yourself. We'll start off with proper communication during planning and charge on toward prioritization, compromises, and a foolproof strategy for staying organized. Even if you're much further ahead, this section contains helpful tidbits that are pertinent to every aspect of your planning journey.

Part II—Budgeting, your lifejacket. This deep dive will help you combat the vastly unfair battle you'll be waging against the wedding industry's asinine pricing. We'll cover your personal financial situation, major wedding costs, and how to construct a wedding budget. All these data points will determine how much "wedding" you can afford. We'll also touch on some financial apps, spreadsheets, and where to put your money to work. If you're lucky enough to have a blank check, you can sit this part out.

Part III—Keeping stress in check. Although this book incorporates stress reduction from cover to cover, this part is dedicated solely to managing stress. It also encompasses the broadest array of stress-reducing guidance (duh). Despite the presentation of these tips in the context of wedding planning, you can still use a generous chunk of them well after your honeymoon and joint tax returns.

Part IV—Intermission. A fine time to use the bathroom.

Part V—A time and a place. We kick off the second half of the book by discussing the site where you'll enjoy the fruits of your labor: your wedding venue. There's a litany of tips on everything from choosing a wedding date to what makes a venue "perfect" and the options for legalizing your marriage. You'll also find a list of over 100 specific questions to ask before signing your life away. Finally, this part houses negotiation tips aplenty, with the simple goal of getting more and paying less. And upgraded dessert. Always upgraded dessert.

Part VI—Vendors and feeding frenzies. There's a battalion of vendors who will clamor for a piece of your wedding and it's stressful to determine who's worthy. This section helps you sift through the duds to find your allies. Whether it's tunes that rock, photos that pop, flowers that don't wilt, or officiants who are licensed, we cover it all. We'll focus on what to consider *before* booking to help you make the most well-informed choice. Also, there's food! Everyone loves food.

Part VII—To your headcount, from your guests. No guests, no stress. Unfortunately, no guests means no reception, either. This part is all about your companions, from how many you should honor with an invitation to ways you can demand they save your date. We'll also touch on what the heck you should do with your wedding registry.

Part VIII—Odds and ends. Just like the rage against conformity by high schoolers everywhere, these components don't quite fit into any of the other categories. Here you can find information on decorations, doing it yourself (DIY), and other random wedding inclusions that might tickle your fancy. We'll also briefly review the reason people get married in the first place—the honeymoon.

Part IX—It's the final countdown. Graduation! These are my ultimate words before you spread your wings and fly away... to matrimony. There will be a few notes of wisdom about writing vows, some counsel on the importance of not throwing up, and considerations for your wedding day, including wedding-day photography. Feel free to get a flavor early on and then reread this part as your wedding looms near.

While I obviously suggest you read this literary classic from start to finish, I recognize the necessity for skipping around to concentrate on what's most pertinent to you. Parts I, II, and III will form your steadfast foundation to ensure success for the entire marathon. It may not be what you wanted at first, but I assure you, it's what you need. This is the bedrock of my turnaround process.

Parts V through VIII explore the essentials you expect to find in a wedding-planning book. Read these in whatever order you desire. You can make this like a choose-your-own-adventure novel, except that every adventure is kind of the same and you always wind up getting married. Part IX is your swansong and means you can *almost* cross over to Elysium, or the conclusion of wedding planning, however you choose to express it.

As you see, this book covers the fundamental aspects of planning a wedding, with an important caveat. This is *not* an all-inclusive wedding-planning guide from top to bottom; it will not examine every detail. Looking for a distinctive type of lace for a wedding dress? Need to figure out where your wedding party should stand at the altar? You won't find those answers within these pages.

The reason for this is twofold. First, I'm not a professional wedding planner, so I don't feel qualified to opine on everything. Second, these details change regularly, so a quick Internet search is more efficient.

OBJECTIVE: YOU

This book is just as much about you as your wedding. Perhaps the most useful material you'll absorb from this book has nothing to do with weddings at all. Rather, you may learn how to change your thinking when tackling *any* substantial challenge—including wedding planning.

The wedding conglomerate loves to pontificate all the required steps for a successful wedding. There is never enough emphasis, however, on what I argue is the most crucial part of planning: you! Pat yourself on the back, warrior. This book is for *you*.

I'm looking forward to sharing some ways I shifted my perspective throughout wedding planning because I'm confident they're suited to a wider audience. At the dawn of the process, I was comparing wedding planning to a slow and painful death, and by the end, I likened it to sitting in bumper-to-bumper traffic. My wife says I'm dramatic and there's something wrong with me. Anyway, my wedding ended up being incredible, so all is well that ends well, right, folks?

My objective is for you to plan a momentous wedding without taking years off your life. You deserve that. Even though I survived the raw, consuming I-hate-my-life-right-now, this-can't-be-worth-it stress, it wasn't graceful. Ask anyone. When I finally gained the courage to tell my friends I was writing a book about wedding planning, they asked, "What are you going to title it? *Don't Do It*?" Let my experience and lessons learned the hard way be your Polaris from the get-go. I'm hoping you'll laugh at my expense throughout (you're welcome) and will realize in doing so that things truly aren't so bad.

This book will be a conversation. I'll do the talking and the drinking; you'll do the reading and, well, maybe also the drinking. In fact, I discovered that relaxing with a drink was one of the best ways to get through the strenuous days of wedding planning and to celebrate the little triumphs. I do recognize it's not for everyone. Maybe your opinion of a reward is binge-watching trashy television or playing dress-up. Hey, if it's a positive experience for you, label it self-help.

By the way, I want to take a moment to emphatically state that this book is for you no matter who you are and who you love. I exclusively use the word "fiancé" as opposed to the somewhat outdated "fiancée." This is simply for ease of writing. We're in the 21st century, both in language and common sense. How lucky are we to be living in a society where any two consenting adults can share in wedding stress? If you're planning to get married, I wholeheartedly support you. Period. We're all in this together.

THE FANCY BITS

Sprinkled throughout this book are a few tricks, anecdotes, and cautionary tales that deserve special emphasis for their own reasons:

Stress-Eradication Tips:

Kill the stress, kill it all. These are tremendously effective stress-reduction tips I wish to underscore, you know, in addition to everything else in this book about stress reduction. Use them liberally.

Rob's Hot Take:

These are experiences I plucked from my own wedding-planning safari, and they worked out swimmingly. Feel free to get inspired by (re: graciously steal) these tips as you see fit. That would be my biggest honor.

Look Before You Leap:

Have you ever heard the expression "measure twice, cut once?" This echoes that sentiment, but for weddings. These are the cautionary truths to ensure you don't have a bad time.

Shut Up and Take My Money:

Although a ton of this book covers approaches for saving money, there are certain instances when it makes sense to invest a little extra for the sake of sanity. These are those times.

So there you have it. Those are the cards I'm laying on the table for you. At its heart, this is a holistic wedding-planning and change-your-thought-process book penned by the guy who you (and everyone I know) would least expect to give advice on the subject. I submit this makes me the ideal author for a work like this. No matter your view on weddings, this book will help you thrive as you complete your journey toward wedding bliss.

Now, enough talk. Let's roll.

PART I
GETTING STARTED

"The secret of getting ahead is getting started."

—*Mark Twain, author*

COMMUNICATION

Ah, yes, communication, the quintessential bedrock of any relationship. Not surprisingly, excellent communication with your significant other is paramount to your success in making it through this thing alive.

Does your partner know your overall attitude toward wedding planning? Do they realize you purchased a book that likens wedding planning to passing a kidney stone? Perhaps you fibbed and proclaimed the book was authored by a bubbly former bride. Either way, it's cool, but it's important for you to level with each other as quickly as possible. Holding the stress and negative feelings inside never helped me, and I don't predict it will do much for you except raise your blood pressure, something my doctor friend advised me isn't good.

STAYING ON THE SAME TEAM

At first, I was nervous about revealing to Jen the true depth of my negative feelings toward planning our wedding. What would she say? She exuded excitement when she started to discuss our wedding. Unfortunately, her fiancé, Eeyore, just didn't share the positivity. I thought coming out and expressing my feelings would crush her. I assumed I could handle the negativity on my own and didn't want to drag her down with me. So what was my brilliant idea? Well, I just let my insidious attitude do the talking. I am not a smart man. All this achieved was silly arguments, hurt feelings, resentment, and cynicism. It was a self-fulfilling prophecy of the worst kind.

After one particularly bitter exchange, it dawned on me that I needed to pull myself together, quit being so juvenile, and talk to Jen about everything. Like many others, I often struggle to speak about my feelings. Sometimes I wonder whether the gene for emotional communication is not compatible with the Y chromosome.

Anyway, I sat Jen down, apologized for being a moron, and spilled my heart. I outlined how I felt about weddings and the voyage on which we were embarking. I tried to explain how I wanted to marry her but didn't have the same positive feelings about a wedding. I told her why. Money, saving for a house, stress, work, and centerpieces were all some targets of my blabbering.

I must have sounded like a bumbling fool. Jen smiled and thanked me for explaining myself. Although she didn't share many of my negative wedding views at this point, she still understood my opinion and that was tremendous. She also now recognized why I wasn't being myself during benign wedding discussions. It just took a direct conversation.

PRODUCTIVE, NOT POSITIVE

At the end of the discussion, I agreed I would make a conscious effort to be productive in our future conversations, even if I felt negative or disagreed with her. In fact, one thing I learned early on is that being productive does not mean agreeing or even feeling positive; it can mean being empathetic or doing more research to fully grasp the opposing perspective. It's critically important to be on the same team as your partner during this process.

You don't need to have the same views or inclinations, but you must be on the same side. When I bottled up how I was feeling and provoked quarrels and resentment, I was not on squad Jen *and* Rob. By agreeing to be productive, I agreed to become part of the team. Think *productive* instead of *positive*. This was a theme I latched onto, and it helped immensely. Funny enough, I noticed more glimpses of *positivity* when I concentrated on *productivity*. I trust you will, too.

Would you rather fight 100 duck-sized horses or one horse-sized duck? This age-old question that has dominated lunch conversations and stumped historians for centuries becomes infinitely simpler when you ask it a different way. Would you rather fight 100 duck-sized horses or one horse-sized duck with your partner or without your partner? Just by adding your partner into the equation, the outrageous task becomes remarkably easier. Whether wedding planning for you is fighting 100 duck-sized horses or one horse-sized duck, having your fiancé there to fight with you makes all the difference. Speak to them regularly about your thoughts so you can stay on the same team.

It's equally essential to *listen*—both when your soulmate gushes with

PART I: GETTING STARTED

excitement and when they divulge fears and angst. This might seem like a no-brainer, but wedding planning is a special beast. It's alarmingly easy to get caught inside your head and drift through the motions. Your partner might be dropping subtle hints that you're not picking up. They need as much support through this expedition as you do, even if they have a more positive outlook. Since you've made it this far in your relationship, this is obviously not new for you, but it's worth repeating because it gets quite simple to disregard as the process envelops you.

Listen here, idiot.

Now for an example. It's no secret I made my wedding feelings known throughout our process, and that's stating it mildly. Indeed, the salient facts about me from these past few pages are that I was 30 at one point, survived to marriage, and hated getting there. Neat.

One night when I was chipper about our wedding (those were rare, so I recall this one), I could see Jen was more reserved and dejected than her normal radiant self. I assumed it was because one of our cats got up when she sat down, and that sometimes does it. However, I could see this ran deeper than ordinary feline rejection and asked her what was wrong.

She said she was overwhelmed with stress and questioning whether a wedding was even a good idea for us. I was shocked because it seemed like this appeared out of nowhere, so I asked her why she didn't talk to me about it. She told me that because I was so negative about our wedding, she felt like she had to be the one who remained positive. Otherwise, we would both spiral into the abyss together.

I had no clue, and that killed me. I should have asked for her thoughts more and supported the notion that she, too, might have a negative mindset to overcome. By concentrating a little more on her subtle cues and inquiring about how *she* was doing, I could have avoided this whole debacle. I was a selfish idiot. This was our second breakthrough, and it taught me the valuable lesson about listening.

Do yourself a favor and keep that in mind throughout the journey. It will spare you from needless conflicts and upset feelings. Express your feelings and listen in return—a clear approach to laying a healthy foundation.

YOU CAN HAVE YOUR SAY IN THIS THING (IF YOU WANT TO)

Although wedding planning *is* a partnership, some couples inevitably won't see it that way. Maybe your partner is the bride-to-be who has daydreamed about every facet of her wedding since she was a girl and before chivalry was dead. (For some reason, Jen reminds me all the time that chivalry is dead.) Perhaps your soulmate is the future groom who wants to integrate all the cool parts of each wedding he's been to, like that killer ice luge.

Invariably, one of you will have deeper preferences than the other. You might find yourself in a position where your fiancé will choose to arrange the entire wedding and you'll just have to show up on your wedding day in your Sunday best. That's unlikely, but miracles do happen. You need to discuss this early and reach a consensus. Get on the same page. Communication, remember?

If you're pessimistic about wedding planning, you presumably don't wish to lay out every element of your wedding on your own. Understandable. However, even with all the negative wedding-related sentiments in the world, you can still have a voice if you so choose.

Remember, above all else, you're entering a partnership. Marrying yourself might seem appealing, but it won't earn you a tax break. Therefore, you need a spouse. When your partner is relying on you, demanding to take a back seat will set you up for failure. Again, be on the same team here and support your partner the same way they need to support you. Sometimes that aid will come in the form of offering your opinion on tablecloth colors, even when you literally have no preference whatsoever.

If you're yearning to be involved and even have ideas about what you prefer, wonderful! Please embrace that. Those feelings will keep you in a constructive frame of mind. I was at my lowest point when I told myself I just didn't care anymore. Apathy breeds all kinds of things, not the least of which is pessimism.

Even if your sole preference relates to the smallest minutiae of the wedding, like the font for your save-the-dates, make that opinion known! That's called being productive, and your partner will thank you for getting involved. However, just know your fiancé might explain that Wingdings is not a wedding-appropriate font and you should grow up. It still beats indifference.

PRIORITIES, EXPECTATIONS, COMPROMISES, AND OTHER FUN WORDS

When I was drafting this section, I did a brief experiment on Google. I searched "wedding ideas" and there were 1.31 billion results. Then I searched "happiness ideas"—526 million hits. Even just searching for "happiness" yielded 905 million results. Therefore, it's easier to find a wedding idea than it is to find happiness. It must be accurate because, well, science! Just kidding. Lucky for all of us, wedding ideas and enjoyment are not mutually exclusive, and there's a bundle of ways to discover both. Also, you have over a billion other resources to help you if you decide this book isn't worth it.

My point is this: there are endless ways to have a wedding. Anything you can imagine is possible. Whether you endeavor to execute all the ideas you can conjure is another question, but it *is* possible.

Enter you and your partner. Each of you will have certain priorities, and those priorities will assuredly evolve over time. That is expected. In a similar vein to communication, it's essential to reveal your priorities and expectations to your fiancé up front and tune in to theirs. Are you sensing a theme yet? Let's call it "the talk."

Friendly note: If you and your fiancé are already in tune about your wedding vision, you might prefer to skip to the next chapter, although some of the takeaways here will apply to other planning deliberations. Your call.

WHEN SHOULD WE HAVE "THE TALK"?

The answer to this question is the same one I used to hate hearing from teachers when I was a kid: it depends. This question is completely couple-dependent, but I can give some pointers for what I believe will lead to a successful exchange. If you've been dating your partner for a while before you got engaged, you may have broached this topic already.

Reflect on any off-the-cuff comments said by your partner about a wedding. They usually start with "if we get married, I want our wedding…" or "we need that at our wedding" or "I hope I meet my future spouse soon." Maybe only the third one if you haven't conquered the friend zone. If these sound familiar, your partner is likely ready to talk.

You will get a smorgasbord of advice directly following your engagement. Jen and I were positively inundated. If you step back and consider what people advise you to do, it's actually quite amusing. Usually it will commence by the person commanding you to not even think about wedding planning and to simply enjoy being engaged. *Immediately following that order*, this oracle will start lecturing about wedding planning or asking you what you are considering for your wedding. All you can do is smile and nod here, folks. We found that saying phrases like "we're talking about it and will discuss it when we're ready" sufficed to pull people off our backs. Try it. When dealing with a pestering relative, just announce you're eloping.

At the onset of your engagement, try to avoid getting entangled in wedding planning. There is enjoyment to be had without the added stress of acknowledging the 400-pound gorilla slowly starting to sit on your chest. Make sure you dine at a multitude of restaurants to celebrate for the first few ~~weeks~~ months. The number of restaurants rewarding you with free champagne or dessert purely because of an engagement ring is staggering.

The priorities dialogue will usually signify your transition into the fray. When you think less about congratulatory messages and more about your ideal venue, it's time. Your willingness to discuss all things wedding might not match your partner's. If you get swarmed with questions before you're ready to dive into discussions, it's important to be receptive to your partner's excitement. Gently let them know that you intend to talk about it but need some time. Showing a willingness to talk, just not right at that moment, is miles ahead of being dismissive and will keep you and your partner in tune.

FORMAL OR INFORMAL?

Nervousness is normal before you dive into your wedding, especially if you've never touched on the subject with your partner. What if your preferences are noticeably different from your partner's? What if you want still water at your table and your partner wants sparkling? How can your relationship possibly survive? I kid. Obviously, each of you will have differing wedding opinions. This conference is about discovering these views straightaway.

This conversation can be as formal or informal as you wish. Some couples might prefer to make a night out of it. You know, crack open that bottle of wine you received for your engagement, order in some Italian food, and absolutely go to town on each other. That's my euphemism for discussing wedding planning. By scheduling a date night, you both will have the right mentality for discussion—without surprises. Besides, who doesn't like an old-fashioned date night?

If the informal route is more your style, just ensure you have sufficient time to fully hash things out. Being forced to curtail a spirited discussion before you can resolve anything might do more harm than good. Also, make sure your initial heart-to-heart just features the two of you so you can be fully honest. My conversation with Jen happened a few weeks after we got engaged. We were sitting in an airport, of all places, waiting for our delayed flight. Who ever said romance was dead?

COMING IN FOR THE APPROACH

So the seed is planted, the wine is uncorked, the order from Tony's is placed, and your partner knows you mean business. Either of you can start. The prominent points to explore in this initial discussion include each of your opinions on the following:

- Expectations for wedding size
- Thoughts about the wedding party
- Desired venue/location
- Preferences on timing
- Views on a religious or secular ceremony
- Cost estimates
- Must-haves

There are a few ways you can try to steer the conversation. One is for each of you to touch on your preferences for the essentials. You mention your hopes regarding the size of the wedding and your partner replies with their views, or vice versa. Ditto for cost, timing, etc. until you work your way down the list. No discussions until you cover all the fundamentals. You don't want to endure a vigorous dispute about one issue before realizing you agree on everything else. Remember, this is a 50,000-foot view rather than detailed specifics.

The opposite approach is to have your dialogue as you hit each point. The benefit of this technique is that if you and your partner are adept at compromises and neither of you have vehement preferences about any one point, you'll agree quicker. This will harmonize you both and create positive energy.

The drawback is the possibility of getting entangled on one point and not finishing the conversation. This might be because of a clash, the scary realization that your partner's views are radically different from your own, or, frankly, just too much wine. If it's the last point, you're welcome. If it's the first two, I have your back in the next section. Don't think I'm going to prep you for battle only to abandon you when things get real.

The last method is for both of you to scribble your expectations on sheets of paper and then swap them. A bit different from the other two approaches, this technique is useful because it allows unrestrained honesty. No one needs to fret about altering a verbal answer to assuage an incoming disagreement. Your true answers are transcribed for posterity.

It's simple. You both grab a sheet of paper and start rattling off aspects you want to discuss about the wedding. While I think it makes the most sense to stick to the main ones for this initial review, if you are passionate about a detail, make sure you inform your partner so it makes the list. You should list each of the above points vertically. It will look something like this:

Guest Count

Cost

Wedding Party

Theme

Location

Ceremony

Must-Haves

After you both write the categories, you each take some time to record your preferences and then trade your paper. Once you know each other's answers, you can focus on the larger disagreements without worrying about whether one of you tempered expectations because of the other's initial answer. Honest conversation from the outset.

Don't worry if it feels like you're stumbling at first; this conversation is just a primer. We're going to go through all the above points in detail throughout this book. That will supply the clarity. If you're *still* not sure where to start, here are 10 questions to help get you both in the mood (for discussing your wedding):

What's your dream wedding?

Have you ever pictured your wedding as a kid? What did you picture?

What were your favorite parts of weddings you've been to?

What do you want most at our wedding?

Is there anything you absolutely don't want?

Have you given thought to what we can afford?

What's your ideal time of year to get married?

Have you thought about a smaller destination wedding?

Do you have strong preferences about the ceremony?

Tell me everything that's in your mind right now about our wedding. Yes, literally everything.

KEEP CALM AND MOVE ON

Regardless of your method or whether you slipped into the conversation organically (i.e., no wine needed), you'll notice that matters become serious very rapidly. It's natural at this stage to get overwhelmed. First you chat about guest counts, and suddenly you learn that not only does your partner desire twice the number of guests as you, but he also demands to arrive on a horse-drawn carriage! How much do those things even cost? What if the horses poop during your entrance? Will you smell the rest of the night? Will your guests think you just forgot deodorant? What about the horse driver? Do you have to pay for his plate? Do you have to feed the horses? See, it's easy to spiral out of control.

It's critical to stay calm and recognize this is just an initial discussion. You just need to understand each other's baselines; you won't be booking anything tonight. You will have more than enough time to thoroughly hash out conflicts. The most productive step each of you can take is to be honest about your expectations while being receptive to your partner's.

Without you knowing, your fiancé might have had a dream in mind since she was a little girl. She'll swear she told you about it before, but you just weren't paying attention (you never are). Think about how devastating it would be for her to raise that during this encounter and you just grunt and dismiss it as stupid or too expensive. Remember, receptive, productive, and on the same team.

Finally appreciating your partner's big-picture wedding plans is a leap in the right direction. That leap either leads to relief that your wishes align or new stress because of considerable discrepancies. If your initial desires are the same, congratulations! You win this round. Just acknowledge that each of your views will shift as you research and expose yourselves to all things wedding. Your introductory debate was not a binding, permanent, until-death-do-us-part contract. That contract appears when you graduate from wedding-planning school.

PRIORITIZE AND COMPROMISE

The pesky disagreements are trickier but can nevertheless lead to surprisingly positive outcomes for you as a couple. Let's focus on them. This is where the next fun word from the chapter title comes into play: *priorities*.

I bet there are a collection of "things" you want in your wedding. You might even be tempted to label these as "must-haves." You will have *some* desired inclusion or, conversely, something you *don't* want—even the apathetic folks.

Maybe you genuinely don't care how the wedding turns out and are leaving all the decisions to your fiancé, assuming they are okay with that approach. Even still, I guarantee you will want to try the food and help set the menu. That counts! If you don't even care to try the cuisine, well, I don't like to use the word "hopeless" too often, but I think you understand where I'm going with this. No matter the number of your expectations, thoughts, or preferences—call them whatever you want—you must prioritize them.

This prioritization is essential because your wedding will not encompass the universe of your desires. This can be for countless reasons, including cost, venue constraints, timing, legality, and *compromises with your partner*. That last point is most important, and you can tell because it's italicized. Compromises with your partner! That's the fundamental reason you should prioritize what you want, and *that* is how you will overcome your disagreements.

I don't want you to confuse compromises here as horse trading. Just because you give up your ice luge does not automatically grant you the sushi bar as a substitute. This is about connecting with your fiancé to grasp what each of you most genuinely cares about—and doing your best to include as many of those aspects as possible.

Compromise in motion.

I can give you an example. For reasons of simplicity, money, and less planning, I wanted to have our wedding ceremony on-site with our reception. For me, locating and booking two separate sites and then dealing with the transportation was unnecessary toil and expense. I didn't want to strengthen an already formidable process, especially while grappling with countless decisions early on; I was simply looking to survive.

Jen hoped for a ceremony separate from the reception. We had previously been to weddings with on-site ceremonies, and some of them did not feature, shall we say, the most attractive ceremony space. It was clear these locations were meant for cocktail hour and reception; the ceremony was an afterthought. Jen obviously wanted to have both a beautiful ceremony space and a beautiful reception space. She also preferred not being constrained by only seeing venues that had the option for an on-site ceremony.

When Jen and I discussed this, we immediately recognized we had a disagreement. Based on our initial chat, Jen knew that this was more important to me than it was to her. I think she also sensed my deer-in-headlights look when I first got engrossed in the wedding world and decided to just let me have this one. Either way, our plan was to find an all-in-one venue space. However, I conceded that even if I loved the venue and it was within our budget, one requirement was a magnificent ceremony area. I was willing to fork over a little extra cash or sacrifice one of my other choices to make it work. That was our first wedding-planning compromise and encouraged both of us going forward.

The key is to decide who has stronger sentiments and priorities regarding the debate. Then act accordingly. If you both believe you prioritize something equally, determine what else you can compromise on so both your opinions are valued.

EMPOWERMENT, TOGETHER

As you work through these exchanges, recall that both of you are getting married, so both of you should be heard. Prioritizing and compromising will empower you both like a well-oiled machine. A vast ocean of disagreements awaits you by the time you cross the finish line of this marathon. If you master how to overcome these from the outset, the proverbial light at the end of the tunnel will be much more attainable. Also, that light won't end up being a bus careening right at you.

THE BRIDE IS ALWAYS RIGHT (?)

Everyone knows the expression "the bride is always right." In fact, I bet when you talk with vendors, you'll hear that phrase ad nauseam, usually accompanied by an irritating cackle to show that the vendor is so relatable to you. It's probably also a slogan for the American Association of Certified Wedding Planners, but don't quote me on that.

There's a reason this quote is so ingrained in society. In my experience, the same experience from which I'm writing, brides *generally* care more about weddings than grooms. Look, I know exceptions exist and that's why I said "generally." I don't think it's a stretch, although give me a shout and advise me exactly why I'm wrong if you emphatically disagree. By virtue, the bride's opinion is the beacon that guides wedding planning and, by extension, the wedding.

I trust this is the case for most couples, and it was the case for Jen and me. However, there were plenty of times I gave my opinion on various aspects of the process, either solicited or unsolicited. To her credit, Jen did a fantastic job of at least listening to my opinion before explaining to me why I was wrong. It was an empowering experience. To my credit, there were at least a handful of times that my point of view had (some) merit.

THE BRIDE IS USUALLY RIGHT

My personal experience affirms we should change the quote from "the bride is always right" to "the bride is usually right, except when she's not and the groom is right, but the groom is wondering if it even pays to be right in this situation, so he decides to be smart for once in his life and just shut up." Perhaps "the bride is usually right" for short. Jen was usually right during our process. No, really. There's no trailing joke. She has a supernatural talent for visualizing designs and then delivering that picture to fruition, all without any outside help. I'm constantly impressed.

To my gentlemen readers, as many of us can deduce, the word "usually" implies that there are times when the bride is *not* right. As a future husband and current wedding partner, you're not beholden to point out these situations in real time, but you should carry on with the understanding and anticipation that they will undeniably surface before you say "I do." The best advice I can give you here is to pick your battles. *Being smart is significantly more effective than being right.*

Tactical silence.

Here's a simple trick to help you tread lightly. Be conservative and assume what you're about to broach will start a feud with your partner, even if logic (haha) dictates otherwise. Is calling out your fiancé worth the argument? Is this disagreement meaningful to you and critical to the success of your wedding? If you feel strongly about a choice, speak up and stick to your convictions. Remember, the bride is not *always* right.

If, after judicious scrutiny, you conclude your point is not that crucial, your survivability increases significantly if you just nod and smile. As the famous quote goes from someone undoubtedly wiser than me, "It is better to remain silent and be thought a fool than to speak out and remove all doubt." As Jen can attest, my adoption of this strategy has been miraculous for cutting the stress for both of us during our wedding journey. I like to call it *tactical silence*. It's smart, it's deliberate, and it works. Brides-to-be, please also adopt this as you see fit. Use it liberally.

STAYING ORGANIZED

At some point over the ensuing weeks or months, you'll realize the breadth of what remains outstanding and what you must accomplish before your wedding can even be classified as a wedding. I wish I could lie to you and say this feeling gently drifts into your consciousness and creates a warming sensation, like watching snow fall from the December night sky as you sip hot chocolate and faintly hear the melodic chorus of Christmas carolers in the distance. At that transcendental moment, you feel at peace with the world. You recognize that no matter what transpires, somehow, someway, you're going to be okay.

If your future included that scene, you wouldn't need to read this book and could happily forge ahead, carefree. I also wished that fuzzy feeling enshrouded me when I appreciated the magnitude of what I had left to plan. Unfortunately, that feeling eluded me (and everyone else who planned their own wedding).

You will surely get *a* feeling, however. Let me paint you a more realistic scenario. It's a Sunday afternoon and you're lounging on the couch with your feet up, watching your favorite NFL team. It's a modest reward for a tough week at work. Not only are you relaxed, but your team's players are finally performing like a cohort of well-paid, elite professionals as opposed to the pathetic group of wannabes who always find a way to disappoint you on Sundays. Life is good. In fact, you *feel* good.

Just as you're beginning to fully savor being on the right side of a blowout score line for a change, your pulse thickens and your breathing increases. Your palms start to sweat. In the middle of a glorious Sunday afternoon and for literally no reason, your brain shifts from Sunday fun day to every aspect you haven't yet figured out for your wedding. You drift from wondering if playoffs are a possibility to wondering whether there will be enough hotel rooms for your overnight guests. Then you feel guilty. How *dare* you attempt to relax on a Sunday, the most prime wedding-planning time slot.

If we consider our snowfall analogy from before, the truth is that these feelings hurtle into your consciousness and create panic, like getting pummeled with hail as you lift your face to enjoy what you thought was the shining sun. All of this is happening as you gasp for air and can hear that cackling wedding planner in the distance. I wasn't lying when I told you Jen calls me dramatic—almost every day.

So maybe it's not quite that bad, but the worst part is how your brain will seemingly flip a switch and fixate on your wedding for no apparent reason. It will happen often. Here's the key: how do you turn these feelings into a fleeting thought instead of an all-consuming tidal wave? *Organization*. You will need to be well-organized to keep your sanity and your positive vibes throughout the tribulations of the wedding-planning experience. Staying organized will be your backbone and will allow you to stay calm and separate wedding planning from the other (more enjoyable) aspects of your life. It will keep you sane and healthy.

Early on, I found myself spiraling because whenever I unearthed a remaining task, my brain then kept jumping to new to-do items I had never thought of. My nefarious brain was constantly pointing out new ways in which I was not prepared. I couldn't relax. It seemed like we had so much to do that I was too overwhelmed to do anything. The journey was looking bleak, and before I knew it, the thought of actually finishing this thing rang like a pipedream. So what did I do? I started with baby steps.

HOW A "TO-DO" LIST IS BORN

The first organizational step I took (besides budgeting—but we'll get there) was to write down any wedding "to-do" that jumped into my head. I started with a piece of paper that I kept out in my apartment. Cooking my famous pasta and jarred tomato sauce when I realize I have to figure out a song for the mother-son dance? Write it down. Trying to wrestle a sock away from Lena when I suddenly remember that we need to get our marriage license? Grab a Band-Aid and then jot it down.

It's such a simple concept, but you will be pleasantly surprised at how the basic act of writing your future tasks will alleviate a psychological burden. By putting pen to paper, you're eliminating the stress that will come from forgetting an important detail. Now it's on paper for posterity and it's only a matter of time before you complete it. You just created your to-do list. Take that, evil brain.

SPREADSHEETS, MY FIRST LOVE

Depending on your technology skills, it might be beneficial to upgrade your paper list into a spreadsheet like Microsoft Excel or Google Sheets. Excel is my jam but is also complete witchcraft in Jen's eyes, so I accept that this tip might not be for everyone. Google Sheets is free and has the added benefit of allowing both you and your partner to access your to-do list from anywhere.

This is handy when inspiration strikes while you're out living your best life. I noticed that always being within arm's reach of my to-do list reduced anxiety, as I never had to question where things stood. Maybe I just have trouble with control. In any case, it's up to you to determine if this capability will be helpful or harmful to your stress levels.

By the way, I don't have any interest in what program you use and just listed those as well-known and effective tools. Employing old-fashioned pen and paper to keep organized is great if that's how you roll. The decisive takeaway here is applying a technique that works for you. I will continue with my spreadsheet discussion but just realize that you can do anything I describe by hand; it just may take you a little longer.

SETTING UP YOUR SPREADSHEET

As you continue adding items to your list, either electronically or with your stunning penmanship, you can start improving by adding the status for each item with due dates and/or comments. In your spreadsheet, this will simply be adding additional columns. It will look something like this:

#	To-Do	Status	Comments
1	Rob's tux	In Progress	Made fitting appointment for August 31 @ 9:30 a.m.
2	Welcome bags	Complete	
3	Wedding bands	Incomplete	
4	Jen's hair	Incomplete	
5	Guest book	Incomplete	

This can be as complicated or simple as you desire. The stronger your spreadsheet prowess, the more features you can add, like a drop-down list for your status column. Other than making you seem like a wizard to the technologically challenged, elements like this are not exceedingly important. A quick Internet search will yield legions of free templates you can nab to help you get started.

This is the solution for tracking your progress and remaining organized through the convolution. Incorporate communication into this list by building it with your partner and encouraging them to add to it. By jointly owning this spreadsheet, you can both be productive, even in your own time. This will be one of the most influential tools in helping you successfully plan your wedding and remain positive along the way. I only wish I built mine sooner.

KEEPING TRACK OF PROGRESS

As you progress, you will feel an unmistakable sense of accomplishment as you change the statuses of your to-do list from "Incomplete" to "Complete." Part of the reason I integrated colors into my spreadsheet was to visually track the eventual change from red to green. On the days when you feel deflated about the journey that remains untraveled, glance at your spreadsheet to appreciate how far you've come. Also, when dread unsuspectingly enters your psyche, simply check your spreadsheet to verify you're tracking the remaining items and have a schedule for completion. Easy.

The to-do list is merely a start. Once you get that squared away and enjoy the empowerment that can only come with a pristine spreadsheet, you can continue to develop a full workbook with multiple sheets. Build these sheets gradually as your various needs arise.

For example, unless you're planning a wedding for two, you will need to invite guests. There's a stack of guest information to transcribe, like constantly changing addresses, email addresses (if you're corresponding digitally), and RSVPs. Maintaining a workbook is perfect for this chore.

You'll need your guests' addresses frequently, so keeping them accessible—and *updated*—is paramount. For a point of reference, my wedding workbook started with just a few spreadsheets and ended with about 10 by the time we sent out our thank-you cards. Your mileage may vary.

MI SPREADSHEET ES TU SPREADSHEET

My original workbook included a multitude of sheets, such as a savings tracker, a cost estimate, multiple guest lists, a gift tracker, and venue instructions. While I encourage you to adopt what you're comfortable with, I would like to offer my own upgraded spreadsheet as tribute. The enhanced version is a polished and consolidated rendition of what I relied on when I was in the trenches. Feel free to use it as a template and modify it as much as you desire. I would be honored if my savior also becomes your savior. You can download a (free, duh) copy for yourself at weddingplanningsucks.com.

WRITE IT ALL DOWN AND UPDATE

Staying organized requires a blend of time and effort. Your investment in organization, however, will pay dividends later when matters become more complicated. It's the best use of your time in the early stages. Although easier said than done, remaining organized throughout the process is suspiciously easy so long as you remember the not-so-secret secret: *write it down*. It's such simple advice; I almost fear I'm insulting your intelligence by telling you. Almost.

Begin with your to-do list and keep that updated. Move on to your savings and record what you're saving and what you need to save (much more on that in the budgeting section). Keep track of the essential dates such as when payments are due, when the venue needs your final guest count, and when you must give your DJ or band a list of song preferences.

Using separate sheets of paper works fine as well. No matter how logical you are in your normal resting state, your brain will often mutate into absurdity during wedding planning. This occurs without warning. You will be like a werewolf, except instead of sprouting more hair and enlarged incisors, you'll gain an *Alice in Wonderland* sense of logic. You can help your brain remain organized by scribbling down *everything*.

Wedding-planning organization is purely a function of keeping your spreadsheets or written notes organized, thorough, and up to date. Amid the chaos, I tried to update my spreadsheets at least once daily. When I started doing this, I was finally seizing control of the turmoil. That act alone decimated my stress levels and improved my attitude. You got this.

WEDDING PLANNERS (NOT YOU, THE PROFESSIONALS)

I wanted to pause here to briefly chronicle wedding planners before moving on to budgeting. By this point, unless you have the short-term memory of a walnut, you know I didn't use a traditional wedding planner. Despite not employing one, I did my fair share of wedding-planner due diligence and happen to know a couple wedding planners personally (I don't hold it against them). So I have a general understanding of what they do.

They do that thing we've been discussing. You know, that thing that once made you nervous but you're feeling more positive about as you're reading this book? Yeah, they help with that. They can run the entire show if you want them to and, more importantly, you can afford their (sometimes extortionate) fees.

PLANNERS: FULL-SERVICE, MONTH-OF, AND DAY-OF
Wedding planners can be full-service, month-of, or day-of. These are

exactly what they sound like. Full-service wedding planners take command of the entire process and you usually hire these people at least 10–12 months ahead of time. They hold your hand through everything and coordinate the whole wedding from start to finish. Full-service planners will also negotiate with vendors on your behalf. As you can imagine, this is also the most expensive option.

Day-of coordinators, not day-of stress.

As a surprise to absolutely no one, there is a horde of required coordination on your wedding day. *Someone* must do that labor, and I submit that it shouldn't be you or your partner. You might consider hiring a day-of wedding planner (or day-of coordinator) to run your show. While you're busy getting ready and second-guessing all your life choices, having a conductor in your corner to oversee your wedding symphony can be a life saver. This white knight will coordinate directly with your vendors, your officiant, the venue, and you. They will also handle last-minute emergencies and ensure proper venue setup so you don't have to worry.

Some venues offer a bridal attendant as part of your package to handle the day-of coordination, so don't jump the gun and hire a day-of coordinator if your venue will provide one. Unfortunately, venues will sometimes omit this service but still require that you hire your own day-of coordinator. Thanks, venue. We knew from our venue contract that ours had us covered. If yours does not, I still highly recommend trading some cash for incredible peace of mind and hiring someone to hold the reins on your wedding day. Their cost should be substantially less than a full-service wedding planner (and worth it).

The month-of wedding planner is a cross between full-service and day-of. The name is a misnomer here because a month-of wedding planner will get involved a few months before your wedding. Once you've planned the big picture, they're essentially the professional that will take over and bring your plan to fruition.

By the time you hire a month-of planner, you will have booked all your vendors. It's like one of those crime shows when the local police are putting painstaking work into the crime scene and then the FBI rolls up and says, "We'll take it from here." There is value in shooing your vendors to your planner in the lead-up to the wedding, as this is one of the most stressful times in the whole process. These planners also provide day-of coordination.

Considering jetting down to Mexico to wed at the resort where you first laid eyes on your fiancé? Yep, there are wedding planners that specialize in destination weddings, too. There are even hourly wedding planners who act more like consultants. The lesson? There is no shortage of personnel willing to seize a role in your planning—if the price is right. Which brings me to...

PLANNERS: COSTS, CONTRACTS, AND BENEFITS

Now that you're acquainted with the various wedding-planner offerings, let's meet the downside: the cost. Like hiring any professional, there is a giant range here depending on factors such as your location (thanks a lot, NYC), the experience and quality of your prospective wedding planner, the size and nature of your wedding, and the type of services you're seeking.

Depending on those components, you can be facing a fee of anywhere from $500 to greater than $5000. For some intricate, high-end galas, that number can easily rise to tens of thousands of dollars or more. Woof.

If you're serious about this route, conduct focused research specific to your location and the services you're considering. Beware: a deluge of wedding-planning websites will try to sell you their offerings. Verify there's a contract listing *everything* for which the wedding planner will be responsible. Read that sucker word for word and ask questions if you don't understand something. A written contract should memorialize any verbal agreements.

Ditch the mercenaries.

When considering any prospective wedding planner, do your best to ensure you're hiring an ambassador, not simply a mercenary. We've briefly touched on some of the insane costs involved with weddings, and there's much more to come. With such a lucrative industry comes those who are simply looking to make a buck off your emotions. You need someone who will have your back, pick up their phone when needed, and fight for *you* every step of the way. Not all wedding planners are created equally. Read the reviews and actually speak to these folks (preferably in person) before making a decision. Try to separate those who want what's best for you—and can prove it—from the vultures who only want what's best for their pocket.

A simple cost-versus-benefit analysis can advise you if hiring a wedding planner makes sense. Everyone is busy, even without the mammoth time commitment that is planning a wedding. Honestly reflect on whether you will be capable of devoting the necessary time to the cause. If you're starting far in advance, this is less concerning for you. If your date is nigh and you're far behind, a planner might bridge that gap. Ask yourself what your time (and stress) are worth here.

Jen and I toyed with bringing in a wedding planner but ruled against it. We based our decision on cost, along with the extensive time until our wedding. It didn't help that we discussed this after I was already white in the face from grasping the obscene prices of certain vendors. *They're just flowers!* We chose to put in the hours on our own so we could save money that would undoubtedly be needed elsewhere. We also knew our venue covered day-of coordination. Discuss with your partner and decide the best answer for your situation.

PART II
BUDGETING, YOUR LIFEJACKET

"Look, I love two industries very much: I love weddings, and I love people dying. You know why? Because when both of those happen, people make stupid decisions. Emotional decisions, not financial decisions."

—Kevin O'Leary, businessman and TV personality

By far my highest priority during the rat race was not breaking the bank. As I've mentioned before, the cost of weddings steered me down the bleak path of pessimism. Dropping a fortune on weddings made little sense to me then and it still doesn't now, even as I revel in post-wedding nirvana. Although Jen shared my viewpoint, she was more flexible and was a proponent of investing in a (hopefully) once-in-a-lifetime experience. No surprise there.

As a numbers guy, I was excited to pen this part. As a wedding-planning survivor, it triggered my PTSD. Weddings are costly. I know that, you know that, and the wedding industry joyfully knows that. I still cannot tell you why venues will impose an arbitrary administrative fee on top of every single line item. For us, it was 20%. Since it's not a tip, what exactly is this money going toward? Why am I paying that 20% fee for both meals and for having the ceremony on-site?

Venues and vendors will charge fees like this simply because they can. As I have learned, do not try to find logic in the cost of weddings, because you will find none. This is particularly strenuous for us analytical thinkers. You just have to accept the absurdity and do your best to save cash where you can. I'll help you do both.

You already performed the first step of budgeting when you exchanged wedding expectations with your partner. Use the number you discussed as your starting point. At this stage, your budget is nothing more than numbers you've jotted down on a page and are striving to stay under. That's it. It's up to you as a couple to be disciplined so you don't blow the budget and to be flexible so you don't become too rigid about each line item. Discipline didn't trouble me. The flexibility? Just one of the many reasons my process sucked.

Try to embrace the budget chaos up front. Your budget is likely going to change (re: go up) throughout the process. Your flexibility will determine how the pandemonium affects you. Visualizing this early will slash your stress later and safeguard your positive attitude. Unlike me, you will prepare for it and you will be ready.

Your budget number is how much you are amenable to spending on a wedding. Because it's ridiculously difficult to estimate all your wedding expenses early on, it's better to begin by concentrating on what you can afford. This is a clearer picture. Peek at your bank accounts and establish what, if anything, you will devote to your wedding. It might be tempting to forgo paying rent for the sake of funding a wedding, but that's just stupid. You have plenty of occasions in your life to be stupid, but financial planning is not one of them.

Now, look at your budget number. If the budget-to-bank-account comparison colors you delighted, you can probably skip the rest of this section. If your reaction is "ruh-roh," like mine was, read on.

YOUR PERSONAL FINANCIAL SITUATION

Your financial battle will be forcing the smaller number, presumably your bank account, to hang above zero as you gradually deplete it with each of your expenses. Some days you eat the beast and some days the beast eats you. Thankfully, you have one massive ally here: *time*. Assuming your wedding is not next week, time to save is on your side. Consider it your comrade. In this sense, it's just like your fiancé but without the smart-ass comments.

Because venue and vendor payment schedules typically feature an initial deposit and a series of payments, it's unnecessary to have the required cash in hand before you book anything. As you replace your estimates with actual costs, your overall budget will become sharper, as will what you need to save.

FAMILY MONEY, FAMILY MATTERS

Sometimes, couples will receive monetary assistance from relatives for their wedding. Historically, or back in the old days, as I like to say to my parents, the bride's parents would cover the costs of the wedding. This was probably an easier prospect before the ugly reality of wedding inflation.

The cost of weddings has disproportionately increased relative to inflation, and it isn't even close. This is clear to see. Ask your parents or older relatives what they paid for their wedding. Then plug that number into an inflation calculator to see today's equivalent. You will be shocked and resentful of the wedding establishment. I blame wedding shows. Therefore, footing the entire wedding bill is no longer expected from anyone's family.

Jen and I were both extremely fortunate to get some financial help from both of our parents. They also couldn't believe the cost of flowers. I wonder if my parents regret their decision now that I've written a book called *Wedding Planning Sucks*. Should make for a riveting Thanksgiving dinner conversation.

If you suspect that any of your parents will contribute financially, try to chat with them now. It can be a little awkward depending on your family dynamics, but urgency is the word here because it might considerably influence your budget. It's best to be direct. Beating around the bush and avoiding actual numbers will convolute your finances and may set you up for future panic.

Family matters can be tricky. This is obviously obvious. If a relative donates a substantial amount of money to the movement, they might feel entitled to have a say in the wedding. You both must determine whether this is probable and whether it's an issue *before* accepting the donation. You don't want to be responsible for the great family schism.

STARTING CASH

Sometimes it's hard for me to convert text into a mathematical equation in my head. I was terrible at word problems in third grade. So here is where we are now, in *equation* format:

$$\textit{Wedding Bank \$ + Family Donation \$ = Starting Cash}$$

Whether you have actually received the cash from your family is not important at this time. You are just seeing your financial status. Family usually gives you cash "when you need it." For you, that won't be for a while. We'll still call it "starting cash" for simplicity.

CALCULATING SAVE RATE

The next step is looking at the calendar for your expected wedding date range. There's no need to be exact, and don't fret if the time span is fluid; we'll discuss considerations for picking a date later. For this exercise, your best guess works. Hopefully, this is something you have already taken up with your partner. If not, nothing is more romantic than imagining the perfect wedding date—in the context of finances. We are determining how many months you have for saving. Keep this number for later.

Last, examine your combined *non*-wedding spending per month. You might need to pour a couple drinks for that discussion. Your first goal is to establish how much money is left over from your normal monthly budget for saving. This will inform your second goal: how you should cut other expenses to save more. If you haven't figured it out yet, we are working backward to see how much wedding you can afford. Simply stated,

Money In - Money out = Save Rate

HOW MUCH WEDDING CAN I AFFORD?

If you've been following so far, you've learned some important planning information. Now for the big shebang. We'll approach this calculation from two angles. First, we'll see how much wedding you can comfortably afford. Then we'll go back to your original budget and see how your original monthly save rate compares to your wedding affordability. Let's figure out what you can comfortably afford. This simple calculation is as follows:

Starting Cash + (Save Rate × Months to Wedding) = How much wedding you can afford

EXAMPLE: CHARLIE AND ERIN

Let's break this down using an example that starts at inception. Let's name our example couple Charlie and Erin. Why? It doesn't matter. These are fake people, people.

If you absolutely need to visualize who these lovebirds are, let's just say Charlie is 32, works with older computers, and lives his life just below his parents' expectations, which is A-okay by him. Erin is 28, works in healthcare, and has an unhealthy distrust of people in uniforms. Why is that important? It's not. As fate (aided by online dating) would have it, Charlie and Erin had been dating for several years before Charlie mustered enough courage to propose to Erin. She said yes! Erin and Charlie are getting married! Their parents are decidedly ambivalent.

ERIN AND CHARLIE TALK

Erin and Charlie had their "talk" over a bottle of malbec, and both concluded they expected to pay around $35,000 for their wedding. This seemed like a realistic number based on what their friends had paid. Whether this was feasible, they knew not, for they hadn't yet calculated the numbers. They elected the following weekend to sit down and figure out their budget. For this occasion, they would split a bottle of water because neither of them were in college anymore and the hangover just wasn't worth it.

Erin had been craving marriage as soon as her besties started having weddings, even though it took her an eternity to meet her definite soulmate, Charlie. Because of this, Erin has two bank accounts, one of which she is using for her wedding savings. She's been saving hard and has already amassed $3000. Charlie, conversely, never gave his wedding a thought and has saved nothing for a hypothetical wedding. Of the $8000 in his sole bank account, he estimates he can earmark $2000 immediately for the wedding. Charlie is risk averse, so he conservatively predicts he will need $6000 for living expenses, unexpected expenses, and his new bougie gym membership to finally impress Erin's friends.

Erin speaks with her parents, who reiterate how delighted they are that she is finally getting married to "Chris." This is the fourth time Erin corrects them. Although they might contribute more later, currently they can commit $4000 to the cause. Charlie's folks, still astounded that he managed not to mess this up so far, also agree to help with the financial burden, contributing $5000. This cash is contingent on amaretto being available during the reception. Charlie and Erin, who have nothing particularly against amaretto, agree.

As we move along, I'll add this information to a spreadsheet to help you visualize it and see how pleasant a spreadsheet can make your budgeting experience. This is the fun part, at least for me. Here you go:

Starting Cash

Erin	$3,000.00
Charlie	$2,000.00
Parents	$9,000.00
Total	$14,000.00

Hopefully, you didn't need to pull out your phone to check the calculus. Charlie and Erin have $14,000 to start! Not too shabby, and higher than some weddings cost in total. Don't get discouraged if your financial picture isn't as rosy as our fictitious couple's. This is purely an illustration to aid me with the math; it's *not* a commentary on what weddings should cost. Jen and I didn't have nearly this much to start with, either.

ERIN AND CHARLIE SPRING

At this point in our fake story with our fake couple, it's April. Erin and Charlie have figured out their starting cash and are both eager and anxious to make some major wedding decisions, like choosing a venue and picking the perfect wedding stamps for their invitations. But before those delights, they must decide when they aim to wed. During their expectations discussion, Erin was adamant about throwing a spring fling because it's her favorite season. She also thought it was symbolic to the growth of her and Charlie's new life together.

In terms of timing, Charlie only cared that a snowstorm wouldn't wreak havoc on their plans. Winter was out; spring was in. Because spring encompasses a few months, Charlie and Erin are looking at a wedding in around 12–14 months.

If you know the exact month you prefer to tie the knot, even better. You can be more specific with your calculation.

ERIN AND CHARLIE SAVE

The last thrill also gave Erin and Charlie the most empowerment—their monthly save rate. A mutual friend recently imbued our fictitious couple with some life-changing advice: learning how to budget. We'll call this mutual friend Rob. With the aid of some free financial apps (more on these soon), Charlie and Erin have easily seen their cash movements for the past year.

It was an eye-opening experience, to say the least. Charlie's friends have always called him a coffee snob, and he was embarrassed to see he was spending close to $250 per month at his darling high-end cafés. Charlie's crushing self-realization paled in comparison to his utter disbelief that he could spend so much on coffee.

Erin's spending ended up being more in line with what she predicted. However, she certainly found room for modest but impactful cuts, like foregoing a weekend trip she had been contemplating. After oodles of analysis and honest discourse, Erin and Charlie determined they could each realistically set aside around $500 per month for their wedding nest egg.

ERIN AND CHARLIE MATH

Now we have everything we need for our initial calculation. Here are the variables in our spreadsheet:

Starting Cash	$14,000.00		
Monthly Save Rate	$1,000.00		
Months to Wedding	12	13	14
Total Budget	$26,000.00	$27,000.00	$28,000.00

There you have it. Based on an initial cash balance of $14,000 and a monthly save rate of $1000 per month, Charlie and Erin's approximate max spend is $26,000 to $28,000.

Remember, this is your *preliminary* approximate budget; it's not your final budget and it will likely change. This initial budget answers the question, "About how much 'wedding' can I afford?" It's valuable to learn this answer before you browse venues and tie down vendors—two sizeable chunks of your budget.

EXPECTATIONS COMPARED TO REALITY

After establishing your affordability by plugging in your own figures, remember "the talk" with your fiancé and the cost assumptions you discussed. The most noteworthy purpose of that conversation—from a financial angle—was for you and your partner to settle on costs, at least loosely. Now that you are finally comparing your predicted cost to your budget reality, there is a trio of inevitable outcomes: your expectations are higher than your budget, your expectations align with your budget, or your expectations are lower than your budget. Let's tackle each.

BUDGET IS LOWER THAN EXPECTATIONS

You may not believe me, but all three outcomes are stellar results. I'll start with the obvious. How could envisioning a more lavish wedding than you can afford be favorable? First, it educates you early, well before you make disastrous and sometimes irreversible decisions, like signing contracts with nonrefundable deposits.

Second, it obliges you to have a cheaper wedding. I'm not being facetious here. Sometimes, dreamers envision an astronomical budget because they assume if something costs more, it must be superior. That is categorically false; some of the best weddings I've attended were outwardly the most affordable. By spending less on a wedding than you were expecting, you are freeing up money to go where you need it more. That's just sensible.

Third, recognizing your lower-than-expected budget at the outset will unquestionably lower your stress in the future. There is nothing worse than wanting to have a $30,000 wedding, planning for a $30,000 wedding, starting to make (nonrefundable) bookings for a $30,000 wedding, and then realizing halfway through the process that you can "only" afford a $15,000 wedding. "Only" is in quotes because it still astonishes me how much money society deems is socially acceptable to spend on one night. I digress.

My point is this: designing a wedding you know you can afford is better for your mental well-being than arranging an extravagant wedding without punching the numbers. Otherwise, what you will be left with is an inevitable gobsmacked look. No bueno. It's not what you want to be doing when you're already stressed with figuring out where to seat your colleague who offends literally everyone she meets but earned her invite after saving your life (and career) that time in Vegas.

BUDGET IS AT OR ABOVE EXPECTATIONS

If your initial expectations are at or below your affordability, that's a splendid start. That means that you either (a) got lucky or (b) already knew what you could afford when you had the expectations talk. Both work! The reason I am lumping both scenarios into the same group is because the advice is similar. Notice that the result of the above exercise is how much you *can* afford, not how much you *should* spend. These are two separate ideas.

People mistakenly assume that because they can afford it, they should purchase it. As I've suggested above, expensive doesn't always mean better. You should *not* arbitrarily splash money to make your wedding more expensive just for the sake of it. That's a silly way to spend. However, if you genuinely desire that more expensive upgrade, go for it! Just make sure it's for the right reasons.

Sometimes when people stockpile for one huge purchase, they subscribe to the fallacy that they "lose" the cash they don't spend so they might as well spend it. Unless you are a multimillionaire selecting between a $240,000 wedding and a $250,000 wedding, a $10,000 difference is massive, and you can still ~~blow~~ invest that denaro elsewhere. Don't overspend just because you can.

If we take it one step further, don't be apprehensive about setting your budget lower than you can afford. This way, when certain prices end up being steeper than you initially predicted, the flexibility will already be prebuilt into your budget. I have found this advice invaluable both for wedding planning and general life budgeting. While employing this tip, I haven't gone broke yet, so it must work.

BUDGETING APPS, A LIFE-CHANGING EXPERIENCE

There are a multitude of websites and apps that can assist with your life budgeting, even if you lack the technical experience. I find them more effective than manual budgeting because they tie into your financial accounts and automatically record *every* transaction and financial transgression. No innocently omitting the nights out with friends. These apps will know and will admonish you for not being more responsible, kind of.

Sometimes the expenditures are benign one-offs and other times it's death by a thousand paper cuts. Either way, they will lay bare all your spending. Lastly, they will categorize each transaction and display your monthly spend.

If you've never undertaken this adventure, it's an eye-opening exercise I encourage you to try. When I teach budgeting to my financially unenlightened pals, I look forward to their inevitable epiphany about tracking spending. It's not exaggerating to label this a life-changing lesson. It's one you'll continue using well after reaching your post-wedding salvation.

The monthly categorization is crucial. It lays out every guilty pleasure for you to behold and paints some harsh realities. You both really love ordering takeout, huh? C'mon, when I try to cook in my small NYC apartment, the steam from the stove fogs up my TV. I totally get it. Maybe your budget favors that now, but when you need to divert more cash to savings, will you still be able to?

That's where another prominent feature of these apps comes in: goals. Goals will add an extra category to your normal monthly budget to help you save for a sizable purchase, like a new car, college, or, you know, a wedding. This ensures discipline with your saving and provides confirmation that you can afford to save as much as you're counting on. As those heavy wedding expenses began rolling in, the goals category provided Jen and me some semblance of comfort. We prepared each month, and now, so will you.

Realizing the utility of these third-party budgeting apps, many credit card companies are offering in-house apps linked directly to your credit card. If you fancy this approach, make sure the app also includes a feature for tracking income. Usually income is relatively stable, but if you finally get that fat bonus you were promised, make sure it gets incorporated into your budget. Monetary gifts are another income component that's worth tracking.

MINT AND YNAB

Although there are countless budgeting apps in today's technological world, there are two apps that are, at the time of this writing at least, widely considered the gold standard: Mint (mint.com) and You Need a Budget (youneedabudget.com). I have no vested interest in either app, and (unfortunately) neither company is paying me.

Both apps are similar and *cross-platform*—a fancy way of saying you can access both apps from multiple devices, like your phone and computer. I won't delve into copious detail since you can easily find reviews of both apps online. This is an intuitive duo, so you can get cracking immediately. I have used Mint for several years with divine success, and it was a remarkable weapon in my wedding-planning arsenal for helping me stay sane. Also, Mint is free, so you don't have to worry about budgeting for the budget app.

At the time of this writing, You Need a Budget costs around $12 per month or $84 for the year. However, this reasonable cost buys you added features such as online financial classes. It focuses on a proactive versus historical approach. If these gizmos sound beneficial, do some independent research to see which suits you best. You Need a Budget usually has a free trial period, so you can try out both apps for free. Getting equipped to forever manage your finances might be the best perk to come out of this Herculean journey that is wedding planning—besides, you know, your wedding.

SAFEKEEPING WITH THE FDIC

Isn't it neat when you search for something on your phone and receive targeted ads for it the next day? By neat I mean creepy and agitating, especially if you're looking for "a friend" and don't want continuous popups for $400 cat portraits.

When I was neck deep in wedding planning, I was searching for wedding-related wisdom multiple times daily. As a result, I was clobbered with a blizzard of targeted wedding ads, and I suspect you will be, too. It really makes it a cinch to unwind and not think about weddings.

As I was researching wedding budgeting, I started getting hit with not only wedding ads but also financial ads and even gambling (!) ads. I guess if some poor soul is trying to afford a wedding, their best bet is to throw it all on red and let it ride. Makes sense.

Even though stocks and other traditional investments might seem like a sly approach for growing your wedding bounty, they come with a slice of short-term risk. Imagine if you invested your wedding savings in the stock market right before one of the major crashes that we've suffered in the not-so-distant past? You might have lost 20% in just a few days! Try explaining that one to your fiancé. Better yet, just plan to permanently sleep on the couch.

With such a slender investment horizon (i.e., the time until your wedding), security takes priority over potential reward. Now for a quick disclaimer. This is neither financial advice nor investment advice; this is common sense. If you have questions about your personal finances and investing, seek a registered financial adviser. I'm not one of those specialists. Please don't sue me.

SEPARATE YOUR BANK ACCOUNT

If you haven't already, it could make sense to open a joint bank account with your partner. However, because of the logistical name-change issues after marriage, you might prefer to shelve this until after you tie the knot. Your call. Jen ended up adopting my last name and spent countless hours dealing with social security, the DMV, credit card companies, banks, professional organizations, etc. I know because she informed me *every* time she spent time changing *her* last name to *my* last name. She's a trooper.

Regardless of whether you opt for a joint account, it's imperative to use a separate bank account for your wedding finances. A detached account will permit easy tracking of all your wedding funds with a quick glance. No need to back out any life expenses.

The wedding spreadsheet we already discussed will help you accomplish this tracking. However, keeping your day-to-day cash intertwined with your wedding savings is a recipe for disaster. Unless you have a profusion of discipline and your tracking is spot on, it will be nearly impossible to maintain separation. Why go through the additional work? There is comfort in the clarity that all ins and outs of a bank account are wedding-related.

A separate bank account also allows you to provide a home to unexpected money that fortuitously drifts into your possession. Two examples are cash from robbing a bank and engagement money gifted to you.

Decide for yourself which is more relevant. The account's separation will deter you from spending wedding money on non-wedding amusements. It also makes it simple to assign capital to the cause.

Since you are projecting to only spend what you *should* spend and not what you *can* spend, you will have some leftover cash when the party's over. What better shelter for this dough than a separate account? When you triumphantly return from your honeymoon, this account will magically morph into a house fund, a baby fund, or a parking spot in NYC fund, all without you needing to lift a wedding-ring-adorned finger. Although it may be hard to believe, life continues after your wedding, so effortlessly preparing for your future is a pleasant bonus of a separate account.

INTEREST – EVERY BIT HELPS

If you still need convincing, my last separate-account plea might resonate the most: interest, baby! If you haven't gone bank-account shopping recently, you may be surprised to learn that times have changed with interest rates. Some banks are now offering interest rates that earn you more than the cost of adding guacamole to your burrito bowl, at least outside of major metropolitan areas.

Interest rates fluctuate according to rates set by the U.S. Federal Reserve. What banks present today will contrast from what banks offer in six months or a year. Therefore, luck with timing certainly plays a role. When you dump serious wedding moolah into these accounts for several months or longer, that interest piles up.

Jen and I were lucky to enjoy interest rates ranging from 1.0% to 2.4% while we were saving. We applied the accrued interest to pay a hefty slab of the tips for our vendors. It's free wedding money just for opening the right type of bank account. Even if rates aren't as generous when it's your turn, every bit helps edge the needle closer to your goals.

These cash machines are labeled "high-yield accounts," but searching for "high-interest-rate bank accounts" should do the trick. They can be either checking or savings accounts. Research to ensure there are no maintenance fees and to determine whether any minimum-balance requirements exist. A third-party resource that compares interest rates will help you navigate these details. These should be simple to find online.

Pick a bank that is insured by the U.S. Federal Deposit Insurance Corporation (FDIC) so it truly is risk-free (up to $250,000). Finally, don't forget to work the interest you earn into your budget. After all, it's more wedding bucks! If you downloaded my spreadsheet, you'll see how I accounted for it.

The poorly understood but occasionally more attractive cousin to the high-yield account is the *money market account*—an account that behaves like a savings account with some features of a checking account. Banks and credit unions offer money market accounts, and they tend to feature higher interest rates than checking or savings accounts.

There's always a catch, though. Some money market accounts require a higher minimum balance than checking or savings accounts. They also sometimes have a monthly transaction limit. Money market accounts might not be the choice for you, but I wanted to at least make you aware of their existence so they can join the conversation. In case you're as risk averse as me, fear not; the FDIC insures these accounts as well.

BREAKING DOWN COSTS

If you've been following so far, you know how much wedding you can afford, you're high off the power that comes from demanding control of your personal financial situation, and you've employed a bank to help pay for your wedding. You created an unbreakable foundation that will make the remaining hurdles a breeze. By breeze I mean suck less. You really are in top shape, though. The next step is for us to flip the script so you can start concentrating on your wedding costs.

SLICING THE PIE… OF CASU MARZU

Since everybody boasts a unique wedding budget, discussing costs in terms of dollars and cents might make this section completely irrelevant for some readers. Instead, I believe it's sensible to grumble about costs as a percentage of your overall budget—a piece of the pie, if you will.

However, paying expenses during wedding planning is like the worst part of the worst thing. So instead of using delicious pie to illustrate the exorbitant costs we'll be shelling out to vendors and venues, let's imagine that we're providing them a slice of *casu marzu*. Casu marzu is a traditional cheese hailing from Sardinia, Italy, featuring sheep's milk and fly larvae. It's known colloquially as "maggot cheese."

Is this analogy petty? Absolutely. But sometimes, that's all we have left.

VENUE AND CATERING COSTS

It comes as no surprise that the largest piece of our wedding casu marzu will be devoured by the venue and catering. Expect to spend an average of 45–55% of your budget on your reception. This is an average, people, so don't freak out if you find the perfect venue and it ends up being higher than this percentage. "Wow, that's a high percentage," you might be saying. Yes. Yes, it is. Weddings are expensive, remember?

The good news is that this massive chunk of casu marzu includes a medley of goodies such as the venue rental fee (if applicable), catering rental fees (if applicable), meals, alcohol, cocktail hour, wedding cake, tips, and service fees (not a goodie). Sometimes that percentage can even include the ceremony fee and after-party, if you go down that route.

The bottom line is you should conservatively estimate at least half of your budget will go to your venue and catering. This is important because your venue is usually your first booking and everything else will build off that. If you drop 85% of your funds on venue and catering costs, you better beg one of your friends to photograph your wedding with a phone. Please don't do this. It's okay to surpass that percentage but just consider you might have to cut more elsewhere.

As a quick aside, I have cost-saving tips specific to each wedding aspect in later chapters. So if you're looking for cost-saving pointers for your florist, for example, you can find them in that section.

PHOTOGRAPHY COSTS

Next up are the vendors. I think about the "big three" vendors as your photographer/videographer, your florist, and your DJ/band. Even though their costs are *somewhat* similar, there is still a wide range based on the services you select. Each will obviously want their lump of casu marzu, so let's begin with who tends to be the most expensive: the photographer/videographer.

You can expect to drop around 10–14% of your budget on digital media. If you opt for photographs only, that number will probably be on the lower end or even below that range, as videography is pricey. Because the cost range for photography and videography is not as wide nationally, I'll share a few actual numbers. The average cost nationally is around $2000 for your photography. Key there is "average"—your mileage may vary. Adding videography will almost double that, tacking on an additional $1800 to $2000.

Don't worry, this is also about the point where I poured myself a drink, too. The numbers sound steep because they are. We're planning for this with our budget, though, so don't get distraught. Besides, the photographer and videographer will be the heroes who provide empirical evidence of your wedding-planning triumphs. So they're on your side, even if they demand a hefty dollop of the casu marzu.

FLORIST COSTS

Florists are up next, and yes, *they're just flowers!* Nothing turns an expensive banquet into a full-blown wedding quite like blossoms. Gentlemen, have you ever gone to get your fiancé some roses on Valentine's Day? I assume you have since you're reading a wedding book and not a book on why your girlfriends keep dumping you. Isn't it neat how the price of roses magically skyrockets around Valentine's Day? If you want them delivered, the delivery cost rises exponentially as well. Man, that's so fun! Isn't supply and demand awesome?

Picture that scenario and multiply it by 10. Then you have the cost for wedding flowers. This is the wedding effect. To be fair to these floral engineers, the cost covers way more than flowers and includes various consultations, décor, transport, delivery and setup, and cleanup.

Expect to allocate 8–11% of your budget on your florist and décor. Your cost will depend on a crush of factors, like the number of tables and what the florist will provide in addition to flowers. This is a prime category for cuts if you need the funds elsewhere. More on that later.

MUSIC COSTS

Rounding out the big three is your music—either a DJ, full band, or guest karaoke (don't do this). There is a broad range of costs here because you can expect to pay significantly more for a full band than a DJ. Turns out it costs more for an imposter to belt out "Don't Stop Believin'" than it does to hear the words come directly from Journey, albeit through a speaker.

You can budget 7–15% on your music choices, with DJs and bands being on the lower and higher ends of this spectrum, respectively. Depending on size, experience, and popularity, you can be looking at an average cost of around $4500 for a musical ensemble to get your guests away from the bar and onto the dance floor. On top of this, you also must budget the cost of paying for these hungry band members to eat. With the average band having six members, that's six additional plates (possibly at a lower rate, but still an added expense nonetheless).

On the other hand, the average cost for the DJ to drop some sick beats (or country music) is around $1000. This is for a bare-bones package. Besides just the music, many DJs will have a cascade of add-on technology like strobe lights, personalized light displays, smoke, and photo booths. If any of these elements are crucial to you, consider budgeting for them now because they likely cost extra. Usually a DJ works with an MC, so you only have two additional plates to finance.

EVERYTHING ELSE (COSTS MONEY, TOO)

As you can see, the lion's share of your casu marzu will go to your venue and the big three vendors. Everything else shares the last piece. I'll give you some examples. First, the ceremony category includes location rental (if separate), officiant fee, and wedding rings. Figure around 5% for the full mix.

Next, don't forget about getting paper! No, I'm not speaking about getting money, because in fact you will be doing the opposite. I'm talking about all the stationery for your wedding, like save-the-dates, invitations, name cards, postage, and thank-you cards. Let's throw welcome bags and party favors into this section as well. Another 3–5%.

Last, the star of the show: the tux… and wedding dress. Hearing Jen tell me how much her seamstress was charging for wedding-dress alterations made me wonder if it was too late to ditch the CPA and become a seamstress apprentice, if that's even a thing. This is the dress-to-impress category. We have the almighty wedding dress, alterations, tux rental or purchase, and the bride's beautification process, like hair and makeup. This category is *probably* another 5%, but it could fly higher based on the dress price.

What about the guest book? What about the bathroom toiletries? Wedding license? Transportation? The costs are endless. I've tried to create a list of items you may not have considered. This will save unwelcome budgetary surprises later, and fewer surprises means more tranquility. As you will see below, there is an absolute load of expenses for your wedding. *If any of these apply to you, add them to your spreadsheet and start budgeting for them!*

I recognize that seeing these all at once can be crippling. Coming from the experience of *not* seeing a similar list until well after budgeting, this early slap is in your best interest. Ignorance will not be bliss, I promise. For the sake of future you, rip off the Band-Aid and have a look:

Ceremony

Officiant fee

Chuppah/décor

Church fee

Marriage license fee

Wedding rings

Aisle runner

Microphone

Reception

Flip-flops

Wedding cake

Centerpieces

Meals for vendors

Coat check

Dance lessons

Party favors

Bathroom toiletries

Photo booth

Photo booth attendant

Ensemble

BRIDE

Dress

Alterations

Hair

Makeup

Nails

Jewelry

Shoes

Veil

Spray tan / teeth-whitening

GROOM

Tux/suit

Cuff links

Tie / bow tie

Shoes

Spray tan / teeth-whitening

Fees

Administrative fees

Sales tax

Stationery

Save-the-dates

Invitations

Thank-you cards

Postage

Programs

Menus

Seating cards

Labels

Gratuities

Captain

Bridal attendant

Maître d'

Bartenders

Executive chef

Officiant(s)

Photographer

Florist

DJ / band members

Extra Events

Welcome drinks / dinner

Rehearsal dinner

After-party

Day-after brunch

Miscellaneous

Guest book

Flower girl's outfit

Bride and groom gifts (to each other)

Welcome bags

Transportation

PUTTING YOUR SPREADSHEET TO WORK

I don't wear makeup, but Jen gives me unsolicited beauty advice all the time. She implores me I need to learn how to braid her hair and apply her makeup in case she's ever incapacitated. I still don't know what she means by "incapacitated." However, next time she's hungover in bed and we have plans to meet her parents for brunch, I'll ask her if she wants me to apply her eyeliner. I assume that's what she means.

One nugget of wisdom she impressed upon me was the importance of a good foundation. It works for makeup and it works for wedding planning. Congratulations, the financial foundation for your wedding-planning journey is complete! Now the real fun begins.

Depending on your preconceived notions about the difficulty of wedding budgeting, the steps we went over might seem like a decent amount of effort. Consider these steps as an investment in your not-so-distant future. The work you endure now will ensure strikingly lower amounts of stress later. If I had put more effort into budgeting earlier, I'm confident my mental well-being would not have suffered as much. I'm also confident your effort will be rewarded.

It's time to leave the nest and spread those financially sound wings! Now that you're squared away with your budget and spreadsheet, the next step consists of entering actual expenses and tracking each of your contributions. This is an intuitive process; do it however makes the most sense. Once again, I'm delighted to share my spreadsheet (weddingplanningsucks.com), but I also think there is some utility in building exactly what works for you. Whether you use mine, tweak mine, or craft your own, there are a few things you should strive to accomplish:

- **Record every contribution to the wedding bank account.** It's a good idea to make note of who is contributing, both on your spreadsheet and on the bank deposit memo. This is to make reconciling the spreadsheet to the bank account easier, *not* to keep score.

- **Track every expense, both historical and future.** If an expense arises and you didn't anticipate it in your original budget, add it in, no matter how small. Remember Charlie's death by a thousand coffee-snob coffees? Consider making a budget category if those small, pesky expenses get to be too numerous.

- **Check your spreadsheet often.** Keep track of the number of days until major expenses are due so you can ensure you have the required cash.

- **Occasionally compare your wedding bank account balance to your spreadsheet balance.** If you are accurately tracking contributions, expenses, and interest, these numbers should be nearly exact. It will give you peace of mind that you have your full financial picture and didn't miscalculate anything.

- **Don't neglect unexpected contributions and interest.** Gifted some cash for your engagement and aim to spend it on your wedding? Make sure it hits your spreadsheet so you can allocate it and put it to work. The interest might not seem significant at first, but it also needs a home on your spreadsheet.

Your budget spreadsheet is a breathing document, so don't hesitate to amend it as your estimated expenses become clearer. In fact, the best practice is to make frequent updates so you have the most current financial picture—both on paper and in your head.

AUTOMATE THE PROCESS

The more you can automate your spreadsheet, the easier your life will be. Hopefully at least one of you has some experience with spreadsheets. If not, there are tons of resources online that teach formula basics. Also, I'm sure there's a friend somewhere who slaves over spreadsheets at work and would be happy to teach you. The acceptable payment for that service is pizza and/or beer.

After you build your spreadsheet, you can tweak it so when you enter a contribution, the total contributions, amount remaining, and account balance all update automatically. Depending on your technical skills, you can add some helpful features like calculating the amount each of you must contribute per month to stay on track. That way, if (and likely when) you go astray, a clear picture will show you how to steady the ship. Again, some of these features are built into my example spreadsheet, so don't hesitate to commandeer them.

THE PERFECT BUDGET AND OTHER FAIRY TALES

The annoying reality is that even if you spend hours on your budget and create a financial command center, all it takes is one big change to throw you in the red. *Having the perfect budget that anticipates every cost is impossible.* Do your best to make peace with that now.

Fret not. I did not shepherd you through the budgeting advice just to tell you not to bother. Regardless of what wedding planning throws at you, bearing a solid budget will keep you well-positioned. You can quickly see the impact to your bottom line and identify ways to mitigate the damage. Hopefully that's reassuring. A robust budget is important when things go right and astronomically more critical when things go wrong.

As my gym loves to say (right above the scale), "Things that get measured get improved!" That's *exactly* the type of content I expect when I drop $50 per month on a gym membership.

OUR "RUH-ROH"

The importance of crafting a budget for when planning goes awry comes from experience. Jen and I created a rudimentary budget in the embryonic phase of wedding planning. Our budget, however, was not robust. We didn't take the time to estimate our cost percentages and what we had to put aside every month. We had an idea of what we assumed we could afford, but that ended up being more of an arbitrary number than a calculation. We eventually figured it out, but not until *after* we booked our venue. You can see where this is going—another ruh-roh.

Yep, Jen and I allocated too much cash to our venue and spread ourselves (very) thin on our remaining budget. As the self-proclaimed numbers guy, I take full responsibility for that snafu. I wish someone had taught us the value of following the steps I introduced above. Instead, we had to learn it the hard way: by experience.

This caused us—specifically me—a *lot* of financial stress. I remember just staring at the venue contract and then my spreadsheet, desperately trying to find a way to make the venue cheaper. Could we omit invitations to the relatives we didn't like? Perhaps a *Survivor* game where the loser doesn't get an invite? Do our guests need to eat? It seemed like a massive weight on my chest. Not good.

NEVER FORGET YOUR PRIORITIES

We had our wedding, and I already proclaimed it was one of the best days of my life. Also, our guests ate. So what was our solution? We went back to the beginning. Remember the priorities discussion? This is the power of that conversation in action. The ceremony and being able to invite all our friends and family were of the highest importance to us. As you recall, I also preferred the ceremony be on-site and Jen requested that it be in a beautiful setting. The venue we chose accomplished all these priorities.

What was not essential? Lavish floral arrangements, extravagant food and drinks, a dazzling light package, and a rockin' band, to name a few.

These would have been brilliant, but they weren't as high on our priority list, so we cut them. Oh well! We reallocated money from areas like vendors and decorations to our venue. Our cost percentage for our venue was now well over the 45–55% range, and our vendor budget also dropped below the "normal" spectrum. Finally, we had to get loads more creative by using DIY items to save money. More tips on those later.

When your budget isn't working, you must somehow scrape together more cash or allocate money between categories. In a world of limited resources, simply maximize what is most meaningful to you and arrange your funding accordingly. Keeping this in mind is the easiest way to stay content with your choices while planning. "Always let your priorities be your guide," said Jiminy Cricket, probably.

Same team, always.

I have one final message to impart before concluding the main budgeting section. This one is more holistic. Budgeting is one of the hardest battles in a difficult war. It might lead to more disagreements and arguing than you're used to. I may sound like a broken record, but make sure you and your partner stay on the same team here, no matter what.

If either of you is adamant about an addition the budget doesn't allow, so what? You'll balance it somewhere else. Your loyalty should be to your partner and not to a computer screen reiterating how expensive weddings are. Don't forgo legitimate feelings for the sake of your numbers lining up exactly. By following all the steps in this section and valuing your partner above all else, you will be victorious in funding your wedding, no matter how small your casu marzu.

PART III
KEEPING STRESS IN CHECK

"Cheer up, the worst is yet to come. Simply put, quit worrying over the little stuff and wait for something really big."

—*Unknown*

Even though stress reduction and positive thinking are part of this book's DNA, I still wanted to devote a section specifically to these pillars. The safeguarding of sanity was glaringly absent from the wedding resources I devoured. Any advice was usually hollow encouragement like, "Try not to get too discouraged—remember, wedding planning is supposed to be fun!"

You can look forward to similar counsel from friends and family when you're neck deep in the bowels of planning. They will make a joke about you losing your mind but won't offer any solutions other than, "Don't stress about this stuff too much. Everything will work out." Wow, thank you for that revolutionary advice. How exactly do I stress less? I think the equivalent is a financial planner advising you to "just get more money." Sage wisdom. This section aims to do more than simply offer the useless platitudes that usually invade wedding books. This is real advice. It works.

I'm going to hit you with a tsunami of different techniques, knowing not all of them will resonate with every reader. The goal is to find a few methods that work for you. If you can do this, the wedding stress won't weigh you down as heavily. Maybe instead of grabbing you around the neck, the stress will just incessantly poke you or put its hands one inch from your face while saying, "I'm not touching you. I'm not touching you." Still annoying, but not particularly harmful. I also think you will find yourself in a healthier place mentally—and maybe even physically.

Aim to learn these coping techniques when you're relaxed. It's far simpler to learn when you're calm than when you're already on edge. Even if you aren't sure whether you'll need to call on these approaches, it's still a good idea to learn them early and keep them in your back pocket, you know, just in case.

Besides not being a professional wedding planner, I'm also not a psychologist. Luckily, psychologists publish their research, and I can read. I was excited to learn from the masterminds who study how we think and am even more eager to share with you the most valuable points. Don't worry, none of this will be too academic, and all of it will be practical. Lastly, I'll have a cheat sheet of sorts at the very end of this section to recap each tip and make it easier to refresh your memory.

MENTAL HEALTH IS ALWAYS IMPORTANT

Before diving into the content, I wanted to add a note here about mental health. Please make sure you take care of yourself and your partner during this process. You should not be feeling so stressed that your physical health is suffering. If you have persistent feelings of panic, hopelessness, sadness, apathy, or general disinterest in the things that normally make you happy, it's time to bring in the cavalry by *talking to a professional.*

It might also be time to make this call if self-help methods fail to reduce stress. Mental health is always important. It's especially important to monitor it during stressful times such as wedding planning. Conferring with a mental-health professional can improve your mood and the ways you cope with stress. Don't try to just "get over it" yourself. Seeking help is a sign of strength, and I hope you also view it that way. You don't have to go it alone.

EUSTRESS VS. DISTRESS

According to the National Library of Medicine, "Stress is a feeling of emotional or physical tension. It can come from any event or thought that makes you feel frustrated, angry, or nervous." So… wedding planning is a synonym for stress? Got it. Planning an event where multiple elements need to coalesce simultaneously will bring you some level of stress, even if you're the most carefree person in the world. It's inevitable.

There's good news, however: not all stress is bad. In fact, in small bursts, stress can actually increase your productivity and ward off procrastination. This is the healthy stress, coined by psychologist Hans Selye as *eustress*. The word literally means "good stress." It might seem like an oxymoron, but science tells us it's not, and we listen to science. Eustress, according to psychologists Mills, Reiss, and Dombeck, has the following features:

- motivates, focuses energy
- is short-term
- is perceived as being within our coping abilities

- feels exciting
- improves performance

The key to success is not to eliminate stress but to use doses of healthy stress for motivation. Eustress is what we're perpetually aiming for. Eustress is the motivation that encourages your productivity and helps you dodge the "oh crap" moment that comes from procrastinating yourself into a panic. Try to utilize it to make progress in your wedding planning.

On the flipside is the unhealthy stress most people associate with the word "stress." This is the stress we're hoping to reduce as much as possible while planning. This *is* the stress with the negative connotation, widely known as *distress*. This is the same "distress" with which you are traditionally familiar. Mills, Reiss, and Dombeck state that distress has the following characteristics:

- causes anxiety or concern
- can be short-term or long-term
- is perceived as being outside our coping abilities
- feels unpleasant
- decreases performance
- can lead to mental and physical problems

Distress is the classic stress we recognize and hate. You know how distress personally affects you. For clarity, when I give you tips on reducing stress, the tips will be for reducing distress, *not* eustress. The most important takeaway right now, however, is understanding that eustress exists. Your goal through this process should be to minimize distress and harness eustress when it arises.

You will quickly learn to recognize eustress. Here's a hypothetical. It's a sunny Saturday afternoon and you and your fiancé are taking advantage of the beautiful weather by people-watching at the park. You see a scruffy-looking man walking his pug and the pug reminds you of one of your fiancé's friends. This makes you realize you still need to confirm several addresses so you can send out your save-the-dates. Instead of continuing to watch Pugsley (because c'mon, what else would we call him?), you get the abrupt urge to pull out your phone and start drafting an email asking these folks for their addresses. The urge comes out of nowhere and it feels *good*. It's not the typical wedding dread you're accustomed to. It feels like your body is summoning you to do this task. Instead of ignoring that impulse, you put it to use. Before you know it, you're ready to press *send*—another small victory.

These are the small bouts of productivity that will keep you on course and productive. On the days when that sudden motivation smacked me out of nowhere, I might spend a couple hours planning, and it felt like nothing. I would just roll down my to-do list and make headway where I could. Often, my productivity would inspire Jen or vice versa.

Listen to these urges and try to be productive with your planning until that feeling subsides. Then stop! Motivation is transient; the trick is to maximize your productivity when your eustress is pumping. It's simple, it makes a big difference over time, and it keeps you from getting burned out.

TACKLING YOUR TO-DO LIST, ONE LAYER OF SNOW AT A TIME

At some point, you will glance at your to-do list and become positively overwhelmed. It happens to us all. When we're confronted with this seemingly insurmountable list, our impetus may be to do nothing because the list is paralyzing. This will lead to a runaway train of stress and negative feelings. What's the best way to halt a runaway train? A snowball, of course.

THE SNOWBALL METHOD

The paralysis from being overwhelmed is not unique to wedding planning. People describe similar feelings when they're plagued by mountains of financial debt. If you ever watch TV during normal working hours, you'll be flooded with commercials about how *you* can get out of debt quickly, followed by about 50 lines of fine print. A popular method for tackling debt is known as the *debt-snowball method*. This idea has been floating around for ages and was made popular by personal-finance guru Dave Ramsey.

For debt, this method involves paying your smallest balances first—the low-hanging fruit. Once you pay off that balance, you take the funds you were allocating to that debt and put them toward the next smallest balance. You continue to gain momentum as you confront each balance from smallest to largest until you pay all your debts. The minor victories in the beginning keep you engaged. By the end, your baby snowball has turned into a snow boulder, capable of destroying your biggest debts.

Now, let me illustrate how sacrificing Frosty will save your wedding sanity. When feeling overwhelmed, scan your to-do list and pluck the low-hanging fruit in terms of effort. What's the easiest and quickest task you can accomplish? Target these first. Center your attention and energy on one task until you complete it. Just one. These tasks can be as tiny as simply making a phone call. Everything counts!

Once you're done, mark that chore complete on your to-do list, changing the color from red to green. This is the start of your snowball. After you slay this initial beast, you can either transition to the next objective or call it a day, depending on your motivation level. Either way, you chipped away at your to-do list. That alone should cultivate positive feelings.

THE AVALANCHE METHOD

Another strategy for paying down debt is known as the *avalanche method*. This is the less popular, scary cousin of the benign snowball. In contrast to the snowball method, the avalanche method is when you first pay off your debts with the highest interest rates, regardless of the balance. Since the higher interest rates generate more debt, you ultimately save money by attacking the higher-interest debt first. The downside to this approach, however, is that it might take you quite a while to pay off your first debt. The lack of early victories could be demotivating, and sometimes those psychological victories make all the difference.

Here's how you exploit this method for wedding planning. Instead of going after the smallest-effort tasks, you aim for the 800-pound gorilla. You know, the grueling line item you've been losing sleep over and the one you quickly scroll past on your to-do list. Even though your conquest might come several days later, the satisfaction of accomplishing such a colossal task will provide the motivational boost your psyche craves.

PICK ONE, PICK THEM BOTH

Consider whether you'd be more receptive to the snowball method or avalanche method. I'm a big proponent of the snowball method; it helped me stay grounded when I would otherwise hyperventilate. Seeing that to-do list change from red to green made a noticeable difference in how I felt. Maybe endorphins? Who knows? I already told you I'm not a psychologist.

You can use these methods in tandem with eustress and distress. When you're distressed but know you need to make progress, focus on a minor chore you'll be able to complete. The act of accomplishing that tiny labor may even jumpstart your eustress. Regardless, that's one task you completed. You made headway despite not feeling up to it—well done!

On the flipside, when you're experiencing a surge of eustress and seeking to be as productive as possible, confront Mr. Gorilla. Use your focused energy and excitement to attack the more effort-intensive tasks, leaving the simple jobs to when you're not feeling as favorable. This allows progress in both states of mind. Slowly but surely, your to-do list will progress from a sea of blood to a field of four-leaf clovers. It's like going from death to... luck? How's that for positive thinking?

"JUST THINK POSITIVELY," THEY SAID

"Just think positively" and "just be happy" were the truisms I received in response to my wedding-planning stress. I'm still amazed at how often I heard those fruitless phrases from engagement to wedding. If changing your mindset purely by "just being happy" was possible, it would render the whole mental-health profession obsolete. Obviously, in the real world, it's infinitely easier said than done. The glass doesn't always appear half full.

Perhaps you'll discover the secret to flipping the happiness switch on command. It seems like Internet advertisements have cracked the code since they herald secrets to happiness all the time (just click here). I'm no conspiracy theorist, but during wedding planning I noticed significantly more targeted advertisements for improving my mood. Now I just get advertisements for life insurance. Hmm.

While I can't offer you any recipe for instant joy, I *can* teach you how to make marked improvements in your mood throughout your wedding-planning turbulence. As always, this stems from personal experience that works.

ACCEPT THE NEGATIVITY

First, how to tackle negative emotions. For the umpteenth time, wedding planning sucks. It just does. Thankfully, it doesn't suck all the time, but it sucked enough for me to write a book about it. It has some element of suck (measured scientifically) for everyone, even those who outwardly had a tranquil time designing their wedding. The dismal outlook *will* enter your mind at some stage, imperiling your directive to "just be happy."

Early on, it felt like I was waging a hopeless battle against these sentiments. When they invaded my mind, I became fixated on them. My brain was seemingly hardwired to highlight every reason this process was rough. First, I considered the cost, and by the end of it, I was pondering how wedding cakes don't even taste that good. Seriously. The more I resisted these notions, the stronger they bombarded me. It's akin to me ordering you not to think about a purple elephant. Don't think about it. Now, is the color of your elephant more of a lilac or plum?

The epiphany for me came more from exhausted frustration than anything else. The initial step I took was to declare a ceasefire and just accept the negatives. Yes, weddings are overpriced, and that's unfortunate. Indeed, there's a flurry of required labor before we get married.

Accepting the negatives when they emerge instead of combating them will help you evade the downward emotional spiral. It might sound counterintuitive, but it worked for me and I trust it will work for you as well. From a logical perspective, I recognized that grappling with negative wedding thinking would impede progress. It's simpler to persuade yourself to accept something for productivity's sake than to constantly harp on it.

JUST THINK (ONE) POSITIVE~~LY~~ (THOUGHT)

The next step is critical, and it's likely what you learn when you click on one of those happiness advertisements. After enabling yourself to accept negative thoughts, *force yourself to think of a positive wedding thought*. Just one. You must be resolute; it's a conscious decision that will demand your disciplined practice. Forcing yourself to conceive an optimistic wedding view, no matter how tiny, will help stem the flow of pessimism. One sanguine thought will often lead to another one. And another one.

Try to never close your wedding thinking with negativity. You can't always control the emergence of negative thoughts, but you *can* control a positive one. Focusing on one cheerful sentiment is inherently easier and more realistic than "just being happy."

If you're having trouble conjuring a positive thought, I can assist. Here's something that's universal to everyone reading this book: wedding planning ends. This basic assurance pulled me through more times than I care to admit. The distress you're suffering is temporary and has a precise end point.

Perpetual worries are abundant in this world. For example, why do we persist with singing "Happy Birthday" when everyone detests singing it and no one enjoys it being sung to them? Why do we still occasionally bite our tongues when we have practiced eating for literally our entire lives? These are illustrations of the *real* worries. I think about them often. Wedding-planning stress? That's just a fleeting burden and will become a memory quicker than you think. Now you might be wondering, should you picture your wedding date as the date you wed or as the date wedding planning is over? Yes.

IT (ONLY) TAKES TWO TO TANGO

In an age when society is constantly pushing the boundaries of social acceptability and legality, it's refreshing to know that marriages are still (usually) between two adults, at least in the United States. Having multiple spouses might sound cool, but imagine needing to plan numerous weddings in quick succession? No thanks. I'm not even going to broach the potential wrath I'd receive for forgetting multiple anniversaries. One spouse is *more* than enough. And, Jen, by enough, I mean perfect.

Because your wedding is for you and your partner only, you both are the stars of the show. Not only are you the main characters, but you're also the entire supporting cast and most of the crew. That means when conflicts arise between you two and someone else, you (as a couple) should take priority 99% of the time. You're the only two protagonists in this Greek trag—err, comedy.

Let's decipher that a bit. Obviously, there is a multitude of other actors who will be involved in your wedding—the wedding party, your parents, your partner's parents, grandparents, friends, ex-fiancés trying to crash the wedding, etc. I'm not saying these folks are not important, but their preferences pale in comparison to yours and your partner's. This is simply not their wedding. They're more than welcome to have their own wedding if they haven't already. Heck, they can plan as many weddings as they desire, just not this one.

FAMILY AND FRIENDS ARE IMPORTANT, JUST NOT AS IMPORTANT AS YOU TWO

In wedding-planning reality, dynamics with family and friends can be taxing. Everyone has an opinion, and unsolicited judgments are readily dished out. Prepare for that now. Usually, these judgments are not nefarious but a way for loved ones to feel included in planning. Sometimes, even when you aren't seeking an opinion, giving an audience to those closest to you will help keep the peace. *If you have no intention of implementing a proposal, listening to the idea and thanking its provider will lead to fewer conflicts.*

A less advisable approach is to explain that you're the star of the show and they're the key grip or teleprompter operator. If dismissing recommendations still gives you anxiety, just remember that by the time the wedding rolls around, it's unlikely anyone will even remember these suggestions. If they question you, point them to the bar and ask if they've tried your signature drink yet.

You have more than enough to worry about (i.e., check your to-do list) without the compounded stress emanating from external criticisms. Declaring that your wedding is between you and your fiancé sounds clichéd because it is. It's also the truth and easy to forget. *There are two people to worry about for wedding preferences—your partner and you.* Carrying this rule as a guiding principle will help you elude unnecessary angst.

If a loved one *does g*et upset, providing an explanation can pacify the situation and help mend hurt feelings. Your rationale need not be more than *gently* stating you don't like an idea. Something like this will work wonders: "That's a really thoughtful idea but I don't think that's the direction for us right now." Another effective mediation is to clarify that you didn't make the choice to purposely hurt someone's feelings. It's nothing personal, fam.

Remember, logic evades *everyone* during wedding planning. If a loved one is being grossly unreasonable, it's quite possible they haven't realized it yet. They will. Wedding-planning lunacy is real and it's universal. *Don't give up on friends and family; they are always important.* Make sure they feel valued during this process, regardless of the role you grant them.

As a final note, don't forget about the budgeting section. If family contributes money to help with the wedding, they might expect to have a voice in some planning decisions. Money is power. Therefore, it's best to converse about their expectations sooner rather than later.

IGNORE THE TV AND THE NOISE

In the same spirit of not getting unsettled by friends and family, I also want to advise you on the dangers of becoming too immersed in wedding culture à la wedding shows and related media. In case you needed the admonishment, *wedding shows are not real life.* They often feature everything from couples with ridiculous budgets (if they have one at all) to celebrity galas with a *team* of planners.

Of course, they can also be wildly entertaining. Jen and I watched our fair share, but our viewing motives differed. Being in a state of exhilaration after our engagement, Jen was seeking wedding inspiration. I, on the other hand, waited patiently for the inevitable drama and tantrums. I was rarely disappointed.

Setting your wedding expectations based on these shows is no different from using the *Fast & Furious* movies as consumer research for your first car as a teenager. For me, reality hit in the form of an old compact that took about 30 seconds to reach 60 mph. My lucrative street-racing career lay in ruin. Profound disappointment ensued.

Thankfully, these wedding shows are nowhere near real life. Expending your energy trying to replicate what you see on TV is a futile exercise. What's the point? We already know you won't stress over your guests' expectations since it's not their wedding, remember? Even if you decided for some bizarre reason that you would fret about how everyone will judge your wedding (you won't), none of your guests are expecting a celebrity wedding, so neither should you. Besides, one of the worst ways to start the next chapter of your life is in debt for the sake of impressing others.

Never lose sight of the fact that you're investing all this effort for a sacred day with your partner. The mythical standards of TV and the judgments of anyone else are just noise. Sometimes the noise can be deafening. However, we do our best to *ignore the noise* and are happier for it.

SOS AND ASKING FOR HELP

"If you need anything, just let me know." How many times have we heard that phrase or been guilty of uttering it without much thought? It's a philanthropic offer when you break down what it means. Unfortunately, this banal saying is often used to politely end conversations rather than offer definitive support. Now when I chat with my friends who are wedding planning, I bid farewell with, "If you need anything, I'm sure it's online." Those poor souls don't understand what's in store for them. Kidding, sort of.

IT TAKES A VILLAGE?

Sometimes it feels like you and your partner may be on an island as you try to work through all the challenges. The two of you aren't alone in this. *Enlist the help of your friends and family to tackle your to-do list.* Contact your squad and ask them to come over and help. Schedule a time and be direct. Because your to-do list is undoubtedly long, there will be tasks ripe for third-party assistance. Suitable candidates are labors you can physically do with someone else, like assembling invitations, cobbling together decorations, or tag-teaming phone calls to potential vendors.

How much latitude you give your ally is up to you. If you entrust them to call vendors, I suggest you have them target the lower priorities. For example, you won't want them booking photographers, but learning preliminary details for rehearsal dinners, organizing after-parties, and exploring day-after brunch options are prime examples of suitable undertakings. As a bonus, spending time with a loved one is refreshing. Enjoyment while making wedding progress? Sounds like a stress-thwarting cocktail.

If you can believe it, some weirdos get excited about the prospect of wedding planning. It's an absurd proposition, I know, but these unicorns exist. There are three reasons people get excited for wedding planning:

1. They're already married and gleeful they can do short tasks without the familiar stress of organizing a full wedding.

2. They aren't engaged yet and don't know better. Also known as the innocents.

3. They love you unconditionally and just want to support you however they can.

Ones bring a mountain of value since they carry advice from the trenches. Use their experience to your advantage. Recruiting a two will bring optimism and reverie. This could be exactly what you need. Heed this warning: you must protect the twos. They're like children who believe in Santa Claus, and you don't want to be responsible for obliterating their fairy-tale dreams with the crushing reality of wedding planning. Tread lightly. Last, the threes. While we embrace any help, help from a three is the best kind of help and usually comes with baked goods and compliments about how handsome/pretty you are.

Acceptable payment for this assistance includes buying lunch for the helpers and inviting them to your wedding. In most cases, do both. Don't forget to sincerely thank them for their contribution and return the favor the next time they could use a hand.

CATHARSIS

You'll experience a wide range of emotions during wedding planning. In other news, water is wet, and pineapple doesn't belong on pizza (come at me). If wedding planning was not mentally taxing, professional wedding planners wouldn't exist. Also, I would have to uncover another harrowing experience to write about, like when I swallowed an apple seed and knew for certain a tree would grow inside me. One of the most effective ways to reduce the emotional distress that stems from wedding planning is to simply purge it.

DEFINING CATHARSIS

The Greek word "catharsis" is a fancy way to describe purging distress. The American Psychological Association (APA) defines catharsis as "the release of strong, pent-up emotions." The science behind the efficacy of catharsis is somewhat controversial, with various scholars holding differing opinions. Professor Emeritus Thomas Scheff (2001) of the University of California, Santa Barbara, made the argument that suppressing emotions had a negative impact on individuals by, among other things, interfering with thought and perception processes.

This is akin to the hydraulic model of psychology. Per the APA (2007), the hydraulic model states, "Emotional distress, if not expressed, gets stored and can create pressure in the system, therefore [sic] 'venting' emotions should decrease tension and consequentially the negative psychological experience and symptoms."

While this school of thought espouses embracing catharsis as opposed to suppressing it, there's an alternate theory that suggests the opposite. Professor Brad Bushman of The Ohio State University studied the venting of anger. He experimented with whether venting anger extinguishes or feeds the flame. His results show "venting to reduce anger is like using gasoline to put out a fire."

Yikes! It's important to note that for this experiment, the "venting" involved participants hitting a punching bag, so bear that in mind. My advice on catharsis for wedding planning involves the release of emotion through communication as opposed to violence against inanimate objects.

RECRUIT "PUNCHING" BAGS

The first method that worked for me didn't involve punching anything. I already mentioned I live in a small New York City apartment, so chances are high I would punch something that isn't meant to be punched and hurt myself. No punching. No kicking, screaming, biting, hitting, or other *-ing*, either, except talking. *The easiest way to release the bubbling stress is to talk through it, often with someone other than your fiancé.* Remember earlier when I avoided talking about our wedding because of how despondent I was? Accidentally stumbling into catharsis was another turning point.

While I vented to Jen early and often, I didn't want to constantly bring her down with my misery. Instead, I recruited a couple of my best friends for venting. Because my two friends were solidly single and had no plans to get married anytime soon, they couldn't care less about planning. That was fine by me.

We went out together one night and I tore into the process, hard. I wasn't seeking advice, but I needed an outlet. My poor friends were my verbal punching bags. After a long tirade, the consensus from my buddies was, "Yeah, that sucks. Let's get more beer." That was the poetry I needed to hear. Yes, it does suck, and thank you for acknowledging it. Even though there was no solution to fix the "suck," just them listening (or pretending to) and acknowledging my concern made me feel noticeably better.

Speak about how you're feeling often. Communicating to your partner is essential, but engaging friends and family has the benefit of a fresh perspective. Borrowing an ear is yet another way to request help from friends and family. Regardless of their response, simply having an outlet will markedly improve the way you feel.

Jen and I spoke to *a lot* of folks about wedding planning. A few people absolutely loved it, and I'm still convinced these lunatics were manufactured in a lab. Unsurprisingly, loads of normal people confessed it was traumatic. Maybe they weren't as close to the abyss as me, but the mental anguish was there. When you're feeling down, remember that even though *you* may be unique, *the way you're feeling is not unique.* There is nothing special about disliking wedding planning. You're in splendid company, and plenty of others have conquered the process before you. Don't lose sight of this.

TO YOU, FROM... YOU.

The second method of release involved me broadcasting my feelings to, well, myself. Seven months and 16 days before my wedding, I started writing in a journal for the first time in my life. Like most of my successful ideas, this one came from Jen. She suggested I invest in a journal so I could write down my feelings and memorialize what I was thankful for. I think she was tired of hearing my constant stream of wedding-related grievances.

I opted for one of those five-year journals where you write a few lines per day. As a journal virgin, I was daunted by the prospect of writing out full-page entries, so I did what any self-respecting person would do—I lowered my expectations. It's much easier to motivate yourself to write a couple of lines before bed as opposed to pursuing a more ambitious literary endeavor.

I unleashed into my journal. *Being able to write whatever I wanted, no matter how objectively ridiculous, was soothing.* The universe of negative feelings stirring in my head was now on paper. Even though only future me would read this, the simple act of memorializing my thoughts felt like a purge. The feelings had to go somewhere—better they go on this page than stupidly stream out of my mouth like usual. I also strived to end my entries with something I was grateful for. I didn't always succeed, but when I did, it helped me refocus on positivity.

The positives need not be life-changing to be effective. Here's an actual entry from my journal: "I wonder how many years this wedding has taken off my life. F***ing awful. I would rather retake the CPA exam than go through this process again. Thankful for air-conditioning." I was a delightful person to hang out with back then. That's just one example.

Family, health, friends, Jen, our cats, and our financial stability are some of the blessings I brought up often in my journal. There are countless bounties in your life, and it's easy to disregard these when you're in a state of distress. Jotting them down is an effective reminder. Even if you can't commit to a journal, try to write these down regularly.

On a daily basis, the five-year journal welcomes you to revisit the previous year. It's an enlightening trip down memory lane, rife with perspective. Those seemingly life-or-death wedding tribulations are a joke now. It's yet another reward you can look forward to when you're on the other side of it all.

Here's the bottom line: if you're stressed about what to offer your guests for dinner instead of worrying about whether you can afford to eat dinner tonight, things are much better than you think. Pause for a second and consider how lucky you are to be planning a wedding. *There are substantially worse reasons to be distressed.* Be thankful for your life's circumstances. While I don't want to downplay the very real nature of wedding-planning stress, a dose of perspective when things get rough is a valuable remedy.

NEVER FORGET THE WHY

On more than one occasion, you'll forget that wedding planning should result in... a wedding. It's alarmingly easy to forget. It's especially easy when you have 20 tabs open on your Internet browser at 11:30 p.m. on a Saturday night and all you have to show for three hours of picking out wedding invitations is that, yes, wedding invitations exist. Why are we doing this again?

Besides inundating yourself with the details of your wedding, don't forget to consider the big picture and remember that the purpose of a wedding is marriage. *You're marrying your best friend.* You and your partner decided to pledge your lives to one another. That's an incredible milestone and should hopefully make you elated. That's always what's most important, no matter how strained you are from planning. Never forget why you're doing all this.

One slight perception adjustment helped my outlook greatly. *Instead of thinking about a wedding as a burden, try to think about it as a kickoff party to marriage.* If the wedding itself doesn't do it for you, focus on the marriage. A small but deliberate change in thinking can have a tremendous impact. Unfortunately, my change in thinking only occurred when my wedding was right around the corner. Don't commit the same mistake. Discover what excites you and make that your motivation.

UPGRADING YOUR RANK

Titles are a sometimes-overlooked perk to your wedding day. I don't know about you, but the title "fiancé" always sounded a tiny bit pretentious to me. Maybe because it's French. In any case, I strongly preferred "boyfriend" and am now perfectly content with "husband." I disliked "fiancé" so much that I used to introduce Jen as my ex-girlfriend. That went exactly as you would expect.

Both "husband" and "wife" are accomplished titles. I think of them like medieval chivalric ranks, like "lady," "lord," or, better yet, "knight." Instead of slaying your enemy in battle, you conquered the far more arduous battle—matrimony—and the grueling process that preceded it. While "fiancé" shows unconsummated commitment, "husband" and "wife" are the real deal. Look forward to that title change.

YOUR LIFE DOES NOT STOP FOR WEDDING PLANNING

Wouldn't it be enjoyable if we could put all the other aspects of our life on hold during wedding planning? No work, no working out, no making dinner, no needing to sleep. What if wedding planning was our only required focus all day? Would that interest you? *Jeez, I hope not.* That sounds heinous. Vile. Repulsive. So repulsive, in fact, it could probably be used as an effective torture technique. Who needs waterboarding when you have vendor calls and seating charts for months? No, I'm not being dramatic; you're being dramatic! Thankfully, life doesn't stop while you plan your wedding. It may seem daunting when other life responsibilities are competing for your attention, but those other obligations will keep you sane.

Not prioritizing wedding planning above all else was one of the few lessons I breezed through. This was the silver lining to despising the process. I never neglected other aspects of my life because almost everything sounded like a more attractive prospect. Need to get a tooth pulled? Why yes, let's make a day of it. Trip to the DMV? I would love to take a number! You get the point.

While my approach bordered on procrastination, I'm not encouraging you to abdicate your responsibilities. I'm advocating for you to continue living your life the way you did before wedding planning. This will protect you from burning out. Even though going out with friends and relaxing on the beach might seem like examples of lower priorities, don't always sacrifice what you love for the sake of checking off your to-do list. Striking a balance between productivity and fun is vital for your mind. Go out. Go on the trip. "I really wish we stayed home to work on our wedding decorations rather than meet our best friends for dinner," said no one ever.

>
>
> ### Tactical fun.
>
> On some occasions when Jen and I were wallowing in wedding torment, we made it a point to stop in our tracks and do something enjoyable. I fondly remember an irritating day when we spent hours figuring out how we would construct affordable centerpieces. I checked the prices of piranhas and fishbowls. They wouldn't be pretty, but they would be entertaining and might even lead to some comical blunders.
>
> After Jen scolded me, we both realized this was pointless, so we stood up, put on our shoes, and went for a stroll. We didn't even know where we were walking, but we knew we needed some entertaining relief. Have you ever people-watched in NYC? It *certainly* doesn't disappoint. In that gratifying evening, we were totally disconnected from wedding stress. You remember tactical silence? This is what I call *tactical fun*. It's effective both as a scheduled pleasure and as an unplanned escape.

HAPPY BODY, HAPPY MIND

Ensure you also continue taking care of yourself while planning. This includes getting enough sleep, continuing to eat healthily when you can, and exercising. While this may seem like common sense, it's staunchly backed up by psychology, and I hope learning the scientific context will help you prioritize it.

Michael Otto, a professor of psychological and brain sciences at

Boston University, told the APA, "The link between exercise and mood is pretty strong. Usually within five minutes after moderate exercise you get a mood-enhancement effect." This mood boost is often immediate. Otto also states that not exercising when you're feeling down is akin to not taking pain medication when you have a headache. Exercise actually boosts mental health, can build the mind's muscles, and can sharpen memory.

And for stress? You guessed it—*exercise plays a significant role in reducing stress and anxiety.* Anthony Hackney, professor at the Applied Physiology Laboratory at the University of North Carolina, found that stress hormones were substantially affected by exercise. People who exercised regularly saw a reduced stress response from those who did not. Physical activity has been associated with decreased symptoms of anxiety and improved psychological well-being in numerous studies. Think twice the next time you skip the gym to work on your wedding. Don't take my word for it—listen to the PhDs!

Not only can exercise help lower your current levels of stress and anxiety, but there are also schools of research that point to exercise *preventing* stress altogether. Dr. Jasper Smits, co-director of the Anxiety Research and Treatment Program at Southern Methodist University, and the aforementioned Dr. Otto studied this. Because the body's physiological reactions to stress are similar to those that are felt during fight-or-flight responses, they theorized that when faced with fight-or-flight situations, those who exercised regularly might become less likely to panic.

Based on their experiment of 60 volunteers with heightened anxiety, those who took part in a two-week exercise program showed significant improvements in sensitivity to anxiety. They did a further study using carbon dioxide–enriched air and found that of all the participants with high anxiety sensitivity, those who exercised frequently were less likely to panic than those who exercised infrequently.

YOU'RE NOT SLEEPING; YOU'RE PLANNING

If your partner is nagging you about sleeping late on the weekend, make sure you jubilantly proclaim that you're preparing for wedding planning. That's because of the strong two-way relationship between stress and sleep. It's common sense that high stress can cause sleep issues. That is anecdotally ingrained in us. The night before finals? The night before a medical procedure? The night before your wedding? See what I did there?

Sleep deprivation profoundly affects our mind. It affects mood, motivation, judgment, and our perception of events. The APA conducted a sleep survey of adults and published some interesting but not surprising results. *Adults who slept fewer than eight hours per night reported higher stress levels than those who slept at least eight hours per night.* Furthermore, adults who sleep fewer than eight hours per night are more likely to report other symptoms of stress, including skipping exercise, feeling overwhelmed, losing patience or yelling at their spouse or partner, and feeling irritable or angry.

Again, sleep is critical to positivity during wedding planning. While the causality between stress levels and quality of sleep is a two-way street, the importance of sleep as a tool to help combat stress cannot be overstated.

FUEL, DON'T FILL

The last component of the stress-reducing wellness trifecta is proper eating. While I encourage Chinese takeout–induced food comas for wedding-planning date nights, just try to eat a salad once in a while. Put your faith in Popeye the Sailor Man over General Tso, whoever that is. Science supports Popeye.

According to professors Michael J. Gonzalez and Jorge R. Miranda-Massari, unhealthy eating patterns result in increased levels of stress. Stress also causes the body to crave foods that are higher in fats and sugars.

A healthy diet can counter the impact of stress and repair stress's damage on the body. Dr. Gonzalez and Dr. Miranda-Massari further tell us that the higher intake of nutrients such as magnesium, iron, selenium, zinc, phosphorus, and calcium, which are associated with high-fiber plant foods, also provides significant stress protection. WebMD also weighs in (obviously the pun was intended) with similar recommendations. Here are some recommended stress-reducing foods for supplementing your lo mein:

- complex carbohydrates (e.g., whole-grain breads, pastas, and oatmeal)

- oranges
- spinach and other leafy greens
- fatty fish (e.g., salmon and tuna)
- black tea
- pistachios
- avocados
- almonds
- raw vegetables (the mechanics of crunching on these can fend off tension)

If you're having sleep issues but still craving a close-to-bedtime snack, try fruit, low-fat yogurt, or a glass of warm milk.

Sad to say, there's an abundance of ways to get enveloped by the tendrils of wedding stress. Many of these factors are outside our control. Diet, sleep, and exercise, however, are mostly in our control. Use them wisely and be deliberate. If munching on baby carrots is an effective way to combat stress, what do you have to lose? Chomp chomp, my friends. Your emotional state will thank you.

THINGS WILL GO WRONG

If you're searching for some spirited wedding-related fun with your partner, look no further than the confines of your abode. All you need is an Internet-enabled device, some alcohol (optional but recommended), and each other. On your device, search for "best wedding fail videos." Just like that, the entertainment will flow.

From entire wedding parties going for accidental swims to revelations about infidelity during the speeches, there is something for everyone. Many a time your eyes will be glued to the screen, and you'll be unable to shake your gaze from the grip of disbelief. I wouldn't call this exercise schadenfreude, per se, but raw astonishment. When watching these videos, remind yourself that an actual human being thought these were good ideas. It boggles the mind.

Besides a heaping dose of amusement, these videos teach us some valuable lessons. First, countless things can go awry during your wedding. They just can, especially with the score of required coordination. Second, of all the possible missteps, some will happen. Call it reality, statistics, fate, karma for laughing at the wedding fail videos, whatever. Somewhere, sometime, *something* will go wrong. It's an eventuality. Do your best to accept it now. *You can lower the chance of miscues through diligent planning. Leave the rest to fate or God or the universe, as it's out of your hands.*

RIP streamers.

Jen and I attended a wedding that featured streamers for everyone to play with during the tail end of the reception. Flailing those things around as the drinks flowed was wildly entertaining. Because of how comical these were, Jen fancied something similar for our wedding. When we dropped them off at our venue, we left the staff with instructions for when they should be brought out.

Somehow, perhaps due to my atrocious handwriting, "please bring these to the dance floor around 10:00 p.m." turned into "please give these to our guests before the ceremony and demand they frantically wave them to welcome the bride and groom." The walk down the aisle felt more akin to a political rally than a wedding. It was bizarre. Thankfully, many of our guests realized the absurdity of the situation and halted their exuberance before Jen made her majestic entrance.

These streamers also never made it to the dance floor. Go figure. No matter how robust your planning and how legible your handwriting, things will go wrong. Although this was just one of many for us, I'm forever grateful our wedding issues were relatively minor and didn't feature a cake tumble—or worse.

IS THIS REALLY THAT IMPORTANT?

As eloquently instructed by the prodigal Van Wilder from the movie, you guessed it, *Van Wilder*, "Don't take life too seriously. You'll never get out alive." This should be the mantra for wedding planning. *In the grand scheme of your life, wedding planning isn't that important. It's just not.* I don't mean this as a dig but a liberation.

On some occasions it absolutely seemed like the most important part of my life, but it wasn't. That realization took me some time. But when I finally got there, the sense of release was palpable. Being able to separate the profoundly important aspects of your life from wedding planning does wonders for your perspective. It's like jotting down what you're thankful for in your journal. I only wish Mr. Wilder's cunning words resonated with me earlier.

Please don't take my advice to mean that your *wedding* is not important. On the contrary, your wedding is a once-in-a-lifetime event. It will be incredible. My point is that you should not hold the act of planning for it in the same regard, especially if it's causing you undue stress.

DO YOUR GUESTS CARE? NO. NO, THEY DON'T.

I have one more slightly controversial truth bomb I've learned from the trenches: *your guests don't actually care about this as much as you do or as much as you think they do.* It sounds harsh, but it's quite the opposite. Think about the components of your wedding for a second. The flowers, the décor, the dinner options, the music—so many of these components are mainly for your guests!

Most of the cash you drop on your wedding is for your guests, so it's no surprise the bulk of the stress will also stem from yearning to impress them. It's a natural thought process. Will there be enough passed appetizers? What is Aunt Marge going to say about the lack of red meat options?

Will Nana be offended by the rap music and the way some of my friends dance, especially Hannah?

Questions like this aren't worth the mental strain. These details likely aren't crossing the minds of your guests, so why the angst on your end? Unless the omission is glaring, like deciding you won't feed anyone, it's challenging for others to picture something that's missing, even if it's at the forefront of *your* mind.

I'll give you a couple examples we grappled with. After learning our venue offered a decadent chocolate fountain as an add-on, Jen was positively smitten. It piqued my interest as well, but I wasn't nearly as enamored. We soon discovered it would be cheaper for us to start our own chocolate company and produce the chocolate ourselves than include the chocolate fountain. Everyone loves wedding prices.

Jen and I went back and forth about this chocolate fountain that must have been made of gold and crafted by Willy Wonka himself. After heaps of budget discussions, we reluctantly opted not to include the chocolate fountain. Guess what? Even though we were disappointed we couldn't swing it, none of our guests seemed to notice that a diamond-encased chocolate fountain was glaringly absent from our dessert offerings.

This perception cuts both ways. While we were contemplating whether to pull the trigger on our eventual venue, the salesperson graciously decided to "throw in" a mashed potato bar for cocktail hour to, you know, really do us a favor. I'm sure our five-digit commitment had nothing to do with it. Mashed potato bars are the real deal, so we were pumped. I remember joking with Jen that even if our centerpieces fell apart and scorched the venue, at least that would be *after* the mashed potato bar. I also faintly recall Jen questioning why I constantly mentioned our venue burning down…

Anyway, the mashed potato bar was at our wedding, or at least we think it was. We didn't actually have time to see it. Because of where the venue placed it, many of our guests didn't know it existed, either. There were photos of it, though, so I guess we'll always have that. The elements you anticipate being spectacular might end up being just a passing murmur to your guests. Don't get too preoccupied with any one aspect of your wedding.

Your guests will have a blast at your wedding. What makes a wedding enjoyable isn't the light package your DJ will try to sell you. It's also not the décor. Sure, the occasional sourpuss will complain about *something,* but that's expected. Reserve the thank-you cards with wrinkled corners for these crayon eaters.

Your guests will appreciate the mountain of thoughtfulness you expended on their behalf, and *that* will be the takeaway at the end of the night (or next morning). If you revel in this fact, the stress about wedding details will be more short-lived than our wedding streamers.

IN CONCLUSION, BAD STRESS BAD

That was probably more than you expected, but I hope you learned something. Again, I don't expect you to harness every pointer here; pick what works best for you. Employing even a few of these tips will make a colossal improvement in your state of mind. I wish I didn't have to learn many of these the hard way, but I'm grateful they're in my pocket for when I deal with my next traumatic endeavor, like buying a house or riding the subway at 3:00 a.m.

These tips are versatile and will come to your aid long after you've "made it" and gotten married. As promised, here is the helpful *CliffsNotes* version or TL;DR (both references for age-inclusivity). Refer back to this list whenever you need a pick-me-up.

- Maximize the utilization of your *eustress* when it arises.
- Adopt either the *snowball method* or *avalanche method* to decimate your to-do list. For greater effectiveness, use both methods in tandem with eustress and distress.
- *Accept the negatives.* Then force yourself to think of just *one positive thought* to stem the negative thinking.
- Remember, the *distress is temporary* and has a concrete end date. Then you get married!
- When you encounter a clash of preferences, *prioritize you and your partner* above all else.

- *Ignore the noise.* Wedding shows are nowhere near real life. Judgments from family and friends are meaningless.
- *Recruit friends and family* to help you overcome your to-do list. You both are not alone in this.
- *Talk through your mental anguish* with a trusted confidant. *Catharsis* releases the bubbling stress.
- Remember, *the way you're feeling is not unique.* Discover solace in knowing this process sucked for countless people before and will suck for countless people ahead.
- *Keep a journal* and use it to write down both the negatives and the positives. Keep your life in perspective.
- Focus on the fact that you will *marry your best friend.* You're planning a kickoff party to marriage.
- *Live your life the way you did before wedding planning.* Don't skip the fun for the sake of productivity.
- *Exercise, eat right, and get enough sleep.* Strengthen the stress defenses you can control.
- Plan what you can but *embrace that things will go wrong.* Don't worry, your guests don't care about this nearly as much as you do.
- In your life's master plan, *remember that wedding planning is an inconsequential blip.*

PART IV
INTERMISSION

"Make your life a mission—not an intermission."

—*Arnold Glasow, businessman*

Now that we've built an impenetrable foundation, it's (finally) time to talk about some logistics. In my humble opinion, the first part of this book is just as crucial, if not *more* crucial, to your wedding-planning success than this second part. Jumping into the logistics without laying the groundwork is how most couples approach the planning process. That fatal mistake is why so many couples end up jaded.

If you already made it through the first half, you're in a substantially stronger position than those stumbling into this process. You're also certainly better off than I was. Perhaps when you pen *your* wedding-venture book, the word "magic" will adorn the title.

Conversely, if you only lay the foundation and don't follow through with bookings, you won't end up planning your wedding. Duh. You will have a neat budget spreadsheet, though, and more money, more time, and probably fewer worries. Wait a second... No! You're having a wedding because it's worth it.

You need to learn to walk before you can run. We took our baby steps earlier. Now it's time to Usain Bolt. I think you'll find a wealth of useful tips here, and as always, I included stress-reduction tips to help you out along the way.

PART V
A TIME AND A PLACE

*"I don't like public venues.
I never know what to wear."*

—Glenn Close, actress

LET'S DATE

The two most important "dates" in your relationship are your first date and your wedding date. Gentlemen, forgetting either will be a bad day. Since I'm probably even more unqualified to enlighten you on dating, let's talk about your future wedding date. You and your partner should already have some idea of timing from your initial wedding discussions. Now we'll dig a little deeper.

Like in most steps, your budget is your springboard. During your budgeting exercise, you calculated your affordability based on the time until your wedding. Never be afraid to update your budget to incorporate planning changes. However, while our budget is a breathing document, selecting a date significantly earlier than the original timeline will lead to a savings shortfall.

If you want an earlier date, make sure your bank account will support the change before you put pen to paper with your venue. Otherwise, you may play financial catch-up throughout the entire planning process—a recipe for stress. Bottom line: your timeline for saving should jibe with your wedding date.

THE WEDDING SEASON(S)

With different seasons come different venue premiums. You will sometimes hear the phrase "peak wedding season" from your prospective venues and vendors. That's wedding speak for "society dictates I can charge more for this because of the date you want." It seems the "peak wedding season" is somewhat subjective and consistently growing to encompass a larger part of the year. Funny how that works.

Generally, peak wedding season extends from late spring through mid-fall, but that's also based on location. For example, summer weddings tend to be more expensive in the Northeast than in the South because of the searing Southern heat. Venues are usually priced by month. The more popular the month, the higher the cost. June and September are frequently the most expensive since they feature the best weather.

Keep in mind, however, that some months seemingly should be cheaper but don't end up saving you cash. Sometimes you aren't competing with Charlie and Erin as much as with holiday parties and corporate events. December is the obvious example because of Santa (or Hannukah Harry, allegedly, as Jen advises me).

Venue slots for the most popular months fill up first (duh), followed by the months surrounding these—the so-called "fringe" months. When Jen and I considered venue dates, we couldn't believe the difference a few weeks made when crossing the fringe. We saved thousands of dollars just by selecting a date in November as opposed to late October. Checkmate, peak wedding season.

These off-peak/fringe months are not only more palatable for venue costs; they'll likely save you money with vendors who play the same pricing games. This treat is often overlooked. When it's time to enter the numbers into your spreadsheet, the overall savings will put the beat-down on your financial stress.

The rest of the costs associated with a date are obvious—the weekend is more expensive than the weekday, Saturdays are the most expensive day of the week, and evening weddings are more expensive than daytime ones. Lastly, winter weddings are the cheapest, but then again, snow stress might be the hardest stress to alleviate.

HOLIDAY WEEKENDS

Undoubtedly, when you start thinking critically about your potential wedding date and how it fits into your budget, you'll think about piggybacking off a holiday. If Sundays are cheaper than Fridays, how about a Sunday before a Monday holiday? Your logic is sound, but before you pat yourself on the back for finding a creative loophole that no one else in the history of wedding planning has discovered, consider that holidays are more complicated than that.

Picture your own traditions for a moment. Whether it's your best friend's annual Fourth of July "beer-be-cue" or your family's Labor Day lake weekend, there are certain red-letter days you won't want to miss. The same will hold true for your guests. Before you commandeer a holiday weekend, take some time to consider whether it will burden them. Everyone knows these holiday piggybacks are cheaper. You don't want your date choice to breed resentment from the get-go and induce an outpouring of RSVP declinations down the line. Just don't push the envelope too far—your guests will appreciate it immensely.

DON'T PLAN FOREVER

When determining the general timing of your wedding, there are a couple of benefits to opting for a more distant wedding date. We already discussed the first: more time to save, so a bigger casu marzu. Second, if you browse venues earlier on, your first choice will probably be available. Something about an early bird and a worm?

As a long-engagement veteran, I want to cast light on something I only considered after the fact. Despite the benefits of our long engagement, a longer engagement inherently means a lengthier period of wedding planning. There's a deeper period of stress and more time for your wedding to hang over your head.

For Jen and me, our engagement length seemed excessive, and we were envious of our friends who opted for a wedding-planning sprint as opposed to a marathon. Just consider this factor before settling on a date. We wish we had. On the bright side, we had more than enough time to positively determine that planning one wedding was enough, so at least we have that.

LOCATION, LOCATION, LOCATION

This is where we start to discuss the big kahuna, head honcho, top banana—your wedding venue. You probably have a lot of questions. These pages have answers. It's far too easy to get overwhelmed with picking a venue and considering the details. Because of this, and in a modest attempt to keep organized, I'm going to break this colossus into multiple chapters. As always, the fabled I-wish-I'd-known-this-in-the-beginning facts are plentiful.

WHERE DO WE START?

I think a better question to ask is, "Where shouldn't we start?" You can find venue inspiration anywhere. As with most questions in our increasingly technological age, begin your quest for knowledge on the Internet. Remember the 1.31 billion hits on Google?

The large commercial wedding websites are the best launching pad. They contain a gigantic population of venues from which to choose and robust filters to hone your preferences. These filters are the bomb. Looking for an affordable, handicap-accessible barn-setting wedding within 50 miles of a specific metropolis? Here are 10 venues that fit the bill. Also, here's the per-person price range, the venue website, a list of amenities, and 100 reviews for you to peruse at your convenience.

It's the most productive way to pare down an overwhelming amount of data. Like many others, we used theknot.com as our starting point and were pleased with the results. Weddingwire.com is another that comes to mind. Try a couple and see which speak to you. The choices are abundant.

If you prefer to trek off the beaten path, your perfect venue might be waiting for you on a wedding blog or user-created site. While stumbling through wedding blogs was the stuff of nightmares for me, it was absolutely Jen's jam and maybe it's yours, too. These sites present inventive venue ideas and can impart wedding inspiration that goes well beyond uncovering a venue.

Nope, nope, nope.

As an anecdotal word of caution, through blogs Jen and I found a couple of venues that didn't appear on the mainstream wedding websites. These locations were also accompanied by some glaring red flags, like unresponsive staff or an unwillingness to even discuss ballpark costs without our visiting, since "you'll have to see it in person to believe the cost." Nope, we're good. Make sure you cross-check these blogs with the mainstream wedding websites, which bestow some level of reputability. At a bare minimum, find independent reviews elsewhere.

IF IT'S A SPACE, IT CAN HOST A WEDDING

Besides traditional catering halls and ballrooms, it seems everyone is jumping into the fray to cash in on the lucrative wedding business. Think museums, castles, aquariums, wineries, botanical gardens, zoos, and even gyms. While it's doubtful some of these ideas made it into your expectations discussion, keep an open mind regarding what's available, especially if you and your partner have an affinity for something unique.

On that note, just because you're picturing your wedding a certain way doesn't mean it's the *only* way. It's like choosing a college. When we sit around with our friends and wallow about grown-up responsibilities, we inevitably start reminiscing about how incredible our lives used to be, before we got to be so lame and our bodies ached for no reason. We gush about college because it was unquestionably the most fun we've ever had. Precisely zero times has anyone said their college experience wasn't the best time of their life because of this nagging doubt they attended the wrong school. It just doesn't happen, folks.

If you're envisioning a rustic wedding masterpiece but can't swing it because (1) it's stupidly expensive and (2) the closest barn to your urban stomping grounds is 200 miles away, the world will not end. You will still find a magnificent venue that ticks all the boxes. Take solace in that point. It will be monumental and sensational—because it's yours.

 ~~Clean your house~~ **Put away your magazines.**

Need a few more ideas for the hunt? Try wedding magazines, vendor recommendations, weekend newspapers, and referrals from friends and family. Be careful with wedding magazines, though. Seeing these lying around the house will make it challenging to disconnect when you need to. They contain a wealth of material and can inspire, but I recommend keeping them stored away and pulling them out only when you're in planning mode. Otherwise, a wandering glance can easily trigger wedding anxiety.

ON-SITE VS. OFF-SITE CATERING

Are you a foodie? Do you describe certain culinary experiences with the same sensual language that must be in *Fifty Shades of Grey*? You've never read it, of course, but you can infer. Are you like me and wish weddings would morph into one endless cocktail hour with passed appetizers? No matter your appetite, catering is paramount to every wedding. There are two venue catering options: *on-site catering,* sometimes referred to as *on-premise catering*, and *off-site* (or *off-premise) catering*.

For on-site catering, the venue provides full-service food and drink options using its own kitchen, culinary team, servers, and bartenders. These costs will therefore be included in your venue contract. If your venue doesn't provide catering—think backyard weddings and wineries—you'll pay the venue a site fee to rent the space (or profusely thank your rich uncle for allowing you to destroy his backyard) and will need to hire a catering company separately.

Purely from a stress standpoint, on-site catering venues are preferable. There's less to plan, fewer vendors to deal with, and less coordination on your wedding day. Plus, the venue lays out all costs at the outset. I'm biasedly a big proponent of this setup for its ease and therefore considerably smaller to-do list.

On-site catering might not be for everyone, though. Perhaps you crave a high-end catering menu that surpasses the typical on-premise venue offerings. Or you may already have a relationship with a caterer and refuse to ingest anyone else's pigs in a blanket. In these situations, off-site catering might suit you better. Reach out to the caterer first before booking a venue to ensure they're compatible.

AT-HOME VENUES–CONSIDERATIONS

While your humble estate may seem like an ideal mix of charm and frugality, there's much to consider before forgoing the traditional venues. Foremost, expect there to be a downpour on your wedding day—even if you live in southern California. Trust me on this one. Expect it with every fiber in your being and plan accordingly.

The hope is, of course, the weather will match the same jovial spirit as the festivities. However, there's nothing worse than being ill-prepared for weather catastrophes. I like to think Murphy's Law was created in the aftermath of a wedding monsoon. Once you confirm your verdant oasis won't mutate into a stiletto-clutching swamp in the rain, you're ready to answer a torrent of other questions:

- **Do you have enough bathrooms?** Unless you reside on a sprawling manor, it's unlikely the bathrooms in your house will cut it. Even if they will, will your septic system? Renting portable toilets is imperative, and we're not talking about porta potties. Think trailers with flushing toilets, hand-washing sinks, mirrors, and air fresheners. Then consider you might need to hire an attendant to tidy these facilities throughout the night. Last, don't forget to ensure your lavatory-on-wheels has wheelchair accessibility.

- **Where are guests going to park?** Will you be hiring a valet service? If there's no parking nearby, will you be providing transportation from the parking site to the reception?

- **Will you be providing transportation to the nearby hotels?**

- **Does your outdoor space have adequate room for an event tent?** Yes, you will need some type of tent or canopy, even if most of your reception is indoors.

- **How is the dance floor going to work?** Can you fit a space large enough for all your guests?

- **Where are your caterers going to set up?** Is there enough room in your house or are you planning on renting a separate space for the caterers?

- **How close are your neighbors?** Will you have any issues with late-night music or rambunctious socialites?

- **Do you need any local ordinance permits?** There are usually a few things you need to clear with your local town or city. Think health department, zoning, and fire marshal. Reach out early to ensure you have adequate time to slice through the red tape.

- **Do you want to get insurance?** Let me help you: yes, you absolutely want to get insurance. We've all seen your friends and what they're capable of. One of your vendors' insurance might cover you. However, talking to an insurance agent about wedding-day coverage and what you might need is a smart move for peace of mind.

- **Will there be someone available to accept deliveries and coordinate setup?** Think tables, chairs, flowers, and décor. How and when is the breakdown going to occur?

- **Who takes out the garbage throughout the night?** Do you have space to put trash out of view from your guests?

After you work through all these questions, it's easy to understand how at-home weddings rarely end up saving you money, time, or stress. My point here is not to disparage at-home weddings. On the contrary, one of my favorite weddings was in a backyard and they might be a marvelous option for you. I'm simply trying to ensure you're prepared for what they entail. In case you're wondering, yes, I did ask Jen whether we could have a 10-person wedding in our apartment. I got a look, but I'm still waiting for an answer.

HOUSE OF WORSHIP VS. ON-SITE CEREMONY

Don't forget that before you get to celebrate the end of wedding planning and, oh yeah, your wedding, you must get married. Like, legally. That's a thing. Where you wed and who officiates your ceremony are deeply personal decisions that will impact your venue selection. Even if you don't revere the ceremony, you still must determine how and where to wed, if purely for logistics.

THE COURTHOUSE

First, there's always the courthouse. Working in lower Manhattan, I pass the New York City Marriage Bureau often and see jubilant couples taking pictures to celebrate their marriage. It's bubbles, flowers, and confetti galore. On countless occasions, I remember jealously gazing at these newlyweds who didn't need to plan a wedding. Ah, those were the days.

If you choose this route, research your state's process to see who can be present for the rite. Also, there's absolutely nothing barring you from knocking out the ceremony one day and then rocking your reception on a different day entirely. While the norm for a wedding is obviously to witness the couple wed, there's no hard-and-fast rule about it. It's your party! Jen and I attended one such wedding reception and remember how enjoyable and laid back it was compared to a more formal affair. If we do this whole thing again (we won't), maybe we'll take this approach (we still won't).

HOUSES OF WORSHIP

If you have your heart set on getting married in a house of worship, such as a church, synagogue, or mosque, there are a few points you should consider early on. Because most religions consider marriage a sacred institution, don't expect to just stroll into one of these places of worship, drop a few Benjamins for a deposit, and wrap up your reservation in 10 minutes. This isn't Vegas, as much as we wish it were.

Finding a house of worship for your ceremony is a considerably more involved process. It usually features interviews with religious leaders and some type of couples' consultation over several months. Also, there might be certain restrictions that only come to light when you finally meet with a representative. For example, rules surrounding the songs you can play in churches are not uncommon. Also, some priests might take issue with what the bride's dress covers (or rather *doesn't* cover). Do your homework early so you're not disappointed or stuck making a last-minute dress change, which, I've been told, is bad.

Another consideration here is obvious: the logistics of using two separate locations on your wedding day. Will guests be expected to drive from your ceremony to your reception or will you provide transportation? What about the out-of-towners? You'll need to arrange transportation for your wedding party, at a minimum.

Furthermore, you need to harmonize the timing. You don't want traffic to limit the time your guests have to stuff their faces with shrimp at cocktail hour, nor do you want your speed-racer friends to awkwardly stand around in the lobby because they screeched up to the venue before they were allowed in. You shouldn't guess here; take a test drive. With the right planning, having your ceremony at a separate location will simply mean a more eventful wedding day. No sweat.

ON-SITE CEREMONIES

The last option is saying "I do" at your reception venue. This means finding a venue that can accommodate a ceremony, cocktail hour, and reception. In some cases, your ceremony and reception might share the same space. In these instances, the venue staff will flip the ceremony area during cocktail hour. This is normal. By the time the space gets reconfigured, the drinks will be flowing and your guests will be too buzzed to notice or care.

As I suggested before, getting married on-site is the easiest option. Less to plan equals easier equals less stressful. That sublime math lesson teaches you why an on-site ceremony was one of my top priorities. You'll also save some cash by forgoing the extra transportation costs. However, the bottom line on price depends more on ceremony fees than anything else.

Don't forget to consider your officiant (the upcoming officiant section helps you do this). Some religious leaders (e.g., Catholic priests) usually won't perform marriages outside houses of worship. If a clergy wedding is high on your priorities list, learn the rules before committing to an on-site ceremony. Otherwise, you'll risk potentially disappointing Grandma.

ALL THE (VENUE) QUESTIONS

As you're neck deep in venue recon, it's sometimes easy to lose your will to ~~survive~~ persist with asking the right questions. I get it because I've been there. In fact, I think I started living there. It's exhausting, it's overwhelming, and there are only so many times you can deal with a salesperson feigning excitement that *you* are getting married. Maybe they actually are excited. I hope they are. It would be nice to find a job where you get wide-eyed and giddy for something you deal with every day instead of wallowing in spreadsheets. I digress.

After paring down your initial venue list based on your preferences, your next step is to reach out to potential venues to both ask follow-up questions and set up a walkthrough. Don't be shy about asking questions ahead of time, especially for venues that are a hike. You have enough on your plate without needing to schlep two hours each way merely to discover your once-dream venue only offers daytime weddings because of "the incident" with the police. The venue did nothing wrong, of course.

If there aren't flagrant red flags that require further investigation, you can schedule a walkthrough. Find out the name and position of the person you spoke with so you can follow up later or in person.

INITIAL WALKTHROUGHS

While the excitement from loved ones may be palpable, I suggest doing the initial walkthrough solely as a couple. There will be plenty of time for gaggles of friends and family to examine the venue and inundate you with questions and opinions. Yes, Grandpa, they have bathrooms. Yep, I'm sure they'll let you sit in the front row for the ceremony.

For now, you want to focus the totality of your energy into the venue to generate an honest opinion, one not colored by the (loving) peanut gallery. You can field questions from everyone later—you know, after you've had a chance to ask them yourself.

The walkthrough is your time. You're the customer and the mantra "the customer is always right" exists for a reason. Revel in it and ask any question you can think of. Don't be afraid to point out anything that gives you pause. Channel your inner NYPD: "If you see something, say something." You're about to be making a major life and financial decision, so you must ensure you have the full picture before doing so.

If your salesperson doesn't have patience for your questions and is trying to rush you along, your warning bells should be ringing. The salesperson needs to be one of the most personable at the venue because their main employment objective is persuading you to sign a wedding contract. The livelihood of the venue and whether it will dine on your casu marzu depends on this. If the salesperson is problematic, what can you expect from the rest of the venue staff?

Am·biv·a·lent.

During the walkthrough, take detailed notes! It's no surprise that Jen nominated herself as our scribe (and adult in the room) while she conferred to me the title of "BS detector." I took my job seriously, and you should, too. If something doesn't feel right, it probably isn't. *Do not compromise if the space doesn't excite you.* While "ambivalent" is a fun word to try to say when you're drunk, it has no place here. There are countless other venues that will give you the warm-and-fuzzies. Don't settle. Remember, you hold all the cards here.

Take incessant photos during the walkthrough. Depending on the number of venues you tour, it's easy for everything to mush into a hazy wedding stew. Match the pictures to the notes for each locale so you stay on track. From a stress standpoint, venue photos allow you to easily share particulars with your friends and family without having to describe every detail, especially when you're exhausted. If any of the venues give you flak for taking pictures, I would be noping out of there real quick as my BS detector goes haywire.

Two > one. Really.

Sometimes, you just need to give the people what they want. It's a safe bet to assume that the people want alcohol—almost always. Therefore, pay special attention to the bar setup. Unless you're hosting a tiny reception, it's *always* prudent to opt for two bars as opposed to one, even if there's an added cost.

Tipsy guests are happy guests, and nothing ruins a party quicker than a game of snake via a lengthy bar line. While a single-bar venue is not a total deal-breaker, at least consider the bar logistics as part of your venue-decision process. At a minimum, inquire about extra bartenders—it's a worthy additional fee.

WHAT TO ASK

Whether you pose questions as you go or wait until the end of the walk-through, try to absorb as much information as your mental endurance will allow. It's perfectly acceptable to leave smaller questions for after you sign the contract if you're satisfied with the big-ticket items.

I constructed a somewhat comprehensive list of questions for you. Considering these issues before signing on the dotted line will spare you a tide of anguish later, especially if any major answers aren't to your liking. In addition to the list below, you can find a printable list online (weddingplanningsucks.com). Feel free to print a copy for each of your venues.

While Jen and I kept some questions in mind during our walk-throughs, having an extensive list would have saved us an onslaught of future phone calls, emails, and stress about unknowns. It seems like future us really resented past us, huh? We're still working on that. Here's the list—remember to breathe.

GENERAL

- What dates are available during our preferred season?
- How do the costs differ for each date? Are there discounts offered for non-Saturday weddings?
- Do you book more than one wedding on the same day? How does that schedule work?
- What is the maximum number of guests you can accommodate? Is there a minimum number of guests?
- Does the maximum number of guests fluctuate based on dinner type (seated vs. buffet)?
- How much is the deposit? Is it refundable?
- Can we reserve without leaving a deposit? How does that work?
- What is the cancellation policy?
- Do you have central air-conditioning or heating?
- Where can we see pictures of previous weddings held here?
- Is there an option for an after-party?
- *For outdoor weddings*: What is the plan for inclement weather?

COSTS

- How are the costs structured? Is there a site fee in addition to the fee per plate?
- Is there an overtime fee? When does it start?
- What is the service fee or administrative fee? Is that fee added to all costs or just certain costs?
- Are gratuities included in the service fee/administrative fee?
- What are the suggested gratuities?

- What is the sales tax? Is sales tax also added to the fees?
- What type of payment methods do you accept? Is there any discount for paying in cash?
- What is the payment schedule?
- What is the plate cost for vendors and children?
- What other possible expenses can be on the final bill other than what we are discussing now?

LOGISTICS

- Is there a separate room for both of us to get ready on our wedding day? When is it available?
- How many restrooms are there?
- Are food and beverages provided to the bride and groom before the ceremony (or entrance, if you are having an off-site ceremony)?
- How does the rehearsal work? Can you accommodate a rehearsal dinner?
- What size tables do you offer? Can you mix and match the table sizes based on the seating chart?
- Are booster seats available for children?
- Are cabs or rideshares easily accessible from the venue?
- What time can each of our vendors set up on our wedding day?
- Do our vendors have to clear everything that evening or can they return the next day?
- When can we start taking photos on our wedding day? Where can we take photos?
- Do you offer lodging? What other hotels are in the area?

- Do you have any relationships with partner hotels that offer discounts?
- How does parking work?
- Do you have liability insurance?
- What are the insurance requirements for vendors?
- Are you wheelchair accessible?

CEREMONY

- Can you accommodate an on-site ceremony? Where can it be held?
- Is there a separate ceremony fee?
- When should the officiant(s) arrive?
- How long should the ceremony take? Will this cut into our cocktail hour?
- What equipment do you provide for the ceremony? Are there added fees?
- What type of sound system do you provide for the ceremony? Is a microphone included?
- Where do the guests go immediately after the ceremony? What about the wedding party?

FOOD AND DRINK

- What are the different food and drink packages and what exactly does each include?
- What types of diets can you accommodate (kosher, vegetarian, gluten-free, etc.)?
- Do you charge for a tasting? What's included in the tasting?

- How many choices do guests have for meals?
- Do guests need to select their meal choice in advance?
- Is the wedding cake included in the food packages?
- If not, is there a cake-cutting fee?
- What drinks are included in the pricing? Are there different tiers of alcohol offerings?
- How many bars are there? How many bartenders per bar?
- Can we set up signature bride and groom drinks? Is there an extra fee?
- Is there a corkage fee?
- Are there restrictions on the types of drinks that are allowed (e.g., are shots allowed)?
- Will you set up the seating cards?
- *For non-open bars*: Do you take credit cards? Is there an ATM on-site?

OFF-SITE CATERING

- Is there a list of preferred caterers you typically work with?
- Are there any special requirements for selecting a catering company?
- What facilities are available for the caterers?
- With whom does the caterer coordinate?

STAFFING

- What staff will assist us on our wedding day?
- Do you offer a bridal attendant or day-of coordinator? If not, is a day-of coordinator required?

- How many wait staff will you provide for dinner service? For cocktail hour?
- Are there room captains? How many?
- Who will we be working with from now until our wedding?
- Will there be a coat check attendant?
- Will there be a valet service? Is this fee included?

MUSIC, DANCING, AND LIGHTING

- What type of sound system do you have? Do you provide microphones?
- What type of connection is there for the DJ?
- Is there adequate space for a band? Is there a limit on the size of the band?
- Who controls the lighting during the reception?
- Is there a late-night music curfew?
- How many people can the dance floor accommodate?
- Can we change the lighting scheme and colors?

DECORATIONS

- Are we allowed to make and bring our own decorations?
- Are there any types of decorations that are prohibited (open flames, glitter, balloons, etc.)?
- Will staff be available to set up and take down the decorations we bring? Is there a fee for this?
- What décor do you provide? Is there a fee to use it?
- What can be moved in each of the spaces?

CONTRACTS AND COSTS

Your enthusiasm will markedly shift as the bubbly amenity discussion makes way for the ominous financial discussion. It's not just your imagination; your salesperson's pupils did just dilate at the mention of the contract. Contracts are their bread and butter and are designed to protect the venue at all costs (pun not intended, but it works, so it stays). Usually, the salesperson will give you a copy to read and sign after you agree on price and inclusions.

As a rule of thumb, the contract should spell out the scope of services, which includes all the salient points, from the cocktail hour offerings down to table place cards. Take your time reading it. It can sometimes be uncomfortable to spend 10 minutes combing through it as the salesperson stares from across the table. Usually, they'll insist you "take your time," but we know they don't mean that, and so do they.

Resist the temptation to bustle through it purely to stem the awkwardness. Embrace the awkwardness. Wear it as a medal of meticulousness. If there's something the salesperson agreed to and your contract doesn't explicitly state it, ask for a new copy with its inclusion. No point is too trivial if it's important to you.

The contract will also include the totality of the financial terms, including the fees and the full schedule of payments. Because your total guest count is still unknown, it should list the price per person, the minimum number of guests, and any discounts for vendors and children—usually after you meet the full-price minimum.

PLUS PLUS – OUR NEMESIS

This is also where you might stumble upon the bane of my existence: *plus plus*. It took me a second to type that because I knew it would raise my blood pressure. Plus plus refers to the arbitrary administrative/service fee and sales tax. Our venue added it to every line item. Literally. Upgraded bar package? Plus plus. Ceremony fee? Plus plus. It's a good thing we love fees and hate money; otherwise, this might bother us.

If you thought you noticed pupil dilation before, just wait until you see the size of those suckers when "plus plus" is first uttered. Unfortunately, we've already established that wedding pricing is asinine, and these stacked fees are just another such example. Understand how plus plus affects your contract. For us, plus plus equated to an additional 28.625%, with the administrative fee being 20% and New York State (supposedly) mugging the balance of 8.625%. *Don't forget to add these fees to your spreadsheet.*

Try not to get too distraught over the preposterous supplemental fees. They suck for everyone. Just chalk them up to the cost of getting married and focus on how you're absolutely going to get your money's worth on the open bar. We're working these fees into our budget so we're fully prepared. Done.

FEES = TIPS?

Find out whether the venue distributes the administrative fee to the staff as a gratuity or if the venue pockets it all. Our contract specified, "For purposes of clarity, the administrative fee is not a gratuity or tip and will not be distributed to any service staff." They must have gotten so fed up with the barrage of questions about random fees that they added this clarifying statement.

While some might disagree with this approach, I found it helpful to ask venues up front about suggested gratuities; I wanted to ensure I was preparing for these in my budget. Our venue offered us a printed list, which was surprisingly light and only included the maître d', the captain, the bridal attendant, and the executive chef. Our salesperson assured us the servers would be taken care of, so maybe the venue shared part of that administrative fee after all. A true wedding miracle. Check out weddingplanningsucks.com for a handy tipping cheat sheet.

THE FINE PRINT

Either at the bottom of the main page or on a separate page, the venue will hit you with their fine print and conditions. Again, read them. If you read something that doesn't make sense, ask the salesperson to explain it in layperson's terms. These terms will outline your responsibility. For example, when your black-sheep cousin decides that punching a hole in the wall is the best way to impress the ladies, you're footing the repair bill.

The conditions should also define what happens if the venue cannot perform its obligations *or if you need to cancel*. This is crucial to read and understand, especially in the wake of a pandemic. If a line in the contract makes you uneasy, there's nothing wrong with consulting a lawyer or confidant before signing your ~~life~~ casu marzu away. The venue should understand this and allow you reasonable time to do so.

NEGOTIATING AND NOT LOSING YOUR SHI(R)T

While you may regard it as inappropriate or even impossible to negotiate with a venue, I assure you it's neither. Since I have a propensity for inappropriate behavior, I submit I'm a qualified arbiter. Furthermore, I know it's possible because Jen and I successfully negotiated with our venue and saved a decent chunk of money in doing so. I trust you'll find these techniques useful to have in your repertoire.

These methods come with the standard caveat that your mileage may vary. It's possible that venues will not provide any wiggle room for a multitude of reasons, even when you lay your best line on them. That's the nature of the beast. Look at successful negotiations as an unexpected bonus rather than a sure shot. That way, you're not too disappointed if you try in vain.

PAY LESS OR GET MORE?

First and foremost, what are you hoping to gain? Since a wedding contract is, in essence, an agreement for you to hand over cash in exchange for a slew of features, you either want to pay less or get more. If you had to pick one, which one is more critical to you? This is your end goal and will dictate the way you approach negotiating. Too often, people concentrate the entirety of their attention on one side of the negotiation—their own. The nature of negotiations is such that each side has differing and sometimes opposite goals.

The same way you hope to keep your wallet full but get heaps of value, venues want you to pay more for less. It's not greed or malevolence; it's capitalism. Tony's would charge $40 for a pizza if they knew you would pony up instead of marching across the street to Classico Italiano's for half the price. As you approach the negotiation table, remember what the venue ultimately wants, even if the salesperson repeatedly declares they have your best interests at heart. That's called sales, and that's the job.

WHAT CAN WE DO FOR YOU?

When you bear in mind the two dueling objectives, figure out what you can offer the venue besides more dough. (We're still doing puns here.) An effective question to literally ask your salesperson is, "What can we do for you?" What are their toughest weekends to book weddings? Are there specific time periods that historically remain vacant? Your negotiating power rises substantially if you have more flexibility with your date. "Sure, I think we could swing that date. If we committed to that day, what could you do for us in terms of the price and offerings?"

Jen and I used this technique, and it got us our wedding date. Not only did we receive a cheaper quote by choosing November over October, but the venue also knocked off an additional $5 per plate because we inquired about their harder weekends to fill. With the cockamamie plus plus, this ended up saving us an added $1000 right off the bat—not too shabby! That money was enough to buy like three extra flowers from our florist.

Another avenue that might bring you negotiating success is the guest count. It's not uncommon for venues to require a minimum number of guests, especially for the coveted Saturday night time slot. If this minimum is lower than your expected guest count, leverage your larger wedding to request more.

For example, imagine the minimum guest count at your prospective venue is 125 guests. Amid the cadre of your work buddies, your gigantic family due to "baby boomers" being true to name, and your fiancé's universe of "best friends" who are really just friends, you know without a shadow of a doubt that your guest count will not be under 175. It's a mathematical impossibility.

Try to exploit this as a negotiating chip. We see your 125 and raise you to 175. "If we guaranteed 175 guests instead of 125, what could you do for us on the cost per plate?" Don't beat around the bush. The bottom line will satisfy the venue, booking a lucrative sale will satisfy the salesperson, and saving money will satisfy you. Give and take—the recipe for successful negotiations.

SWITCH OBJECTIVES

If the venue is pushing back on your primary aim, try the other one. We learned venues are more likely to throw in additional perks as opposed to reducing the overall cost. I imagine it's because of the scandalous markup on most of the options, like the elusive chocolate fountain.

If they aren't budging on the buck, pursue the additional bang. Remember, the venue will still expect reciprocation. If this venue is "the one," make it known you will put down a deposit today if you get immense value. The certainty of a booking today can be enough for the venue to throw in some extras to sweeten the deal, such as upgraded drinks, dessert add-ons, or maybe even that legendary ice luge.

BE COOPERATIVE, NOT COMBATIVE

Although it might seem tempting, resist the urge to go to war over this contract. You don't have to "win" against the venue. Consider negotiating as solving a problem you both have. Your problem is you need a wedding locale; their problem is they need to rent out their space for an inflated price. How can you both make this work?

Maintaining this cooperative mindset instead of a combative posture has a stronger chance of success. Just remember, both sides can play hardball here, and the more popular the venue, the less leverage you have backing you up. Work together, not against each other.

JUST ASK

Finally, you would be surprised what the venue might toss in if you just ask for it. Even if you awkwardly ask in a half-joking manner to save you the discomfort, the worst they can say is no. You really have nothing to lose, except maybe your dignity, but that's long gone, isn't it? The venue wants your business and sometimes that alone is enough for them to make concessions. As a parting reminder, make sure any negotiation triumph gets memorialized in the contract before you sign.

HOTELS

The final venue point addresses your guests' temporary home while they get dressed to kill—the hotel. It will graciously accept them for who they are and provide end-of-night refuge, regardless of the poor choices they made on the dance floor. It might even serve as the locale for your afterparty! The hotel scene is one you must consider before booking a venue.

PARTNER HOTELS

Your initial foray into the area's hospitality options will likely come during your venue walkthrough. Because the wedding coalition features a web of people trying to scratch each other's backs, your venue will be eager to recommend a partner hotel. Your venue might even *be* a hotel. This simplifies the hunt.

Partner hotels usually provide a room block for your overnight guests at a discounted rate. Your venue salesperson will get you in touch with the hotel's sales coordinator to iron out the details. It's your job to ensure a room block for your wedding weekend. Pay particular attention to multiple weddings near your date, as that could mean limited hotel availability for your guests. Offering to fill a set number of rooms at a partner hotel is another bargaining chip you can lean on during your venue negotiations.

Even after you select a hotel, research the availability of other hotels in the area. It's thoughtful to give your guests a few options in case your main hotel is full or too pricey for some. It's a common gesture for your main hotel to give you a complimentary room for the night of your wedding—and possibly even a wedding suite. I suppose that's hotel speak for "thank you."

A place for pants.

Jen and I failed to consider where we would both get ready on our wedding day. While the venue offered a bridal suite, it was tiny and not meant to be used until hair and makeup were complete. To complicate matters further, we adhered to the tradition of not seeing each other until our first look.

By the time we realized our dilemma, the hotel was full. We orchestrated a game of cat and mouse between a couple rooms. It was peachy for me; all I really had to do was put on pants. However, matters were much harder for Jen and her beautification process—a process I'm told all brides subject themselves to. Here's the bottom line: think about logistics for getting ready well ahead of time so you don't add unnecessary stress to your wedding day, like we did.

TRANSPORTATION CONSIDERATIONS

With the consideration for hotels comes the consideration for transportation. Will you be arranging a shuttle to shepherd your guests to and from the hotel? Some hotels might offer this service to entice you to reserve with them instead of with another hotel.

If this route is not in the cards for your budget, you should ensure there are adequate taxis or rideshares available at the venue. Many of your guests will rightfully not plan to drive since they're probably expecting a bender, based on how you behaved in college. Make it easy and *safe* for them after the party's over. It's the responsible thing to do.

EXTRACURRICULARS

On a final note, make sure your hotel choice jibes with any extracurriculars of your wedding, such as the rehearsal dinner, welcome drinks, after-party, and morning-after brunch/breakfast. If your hotel is booked solid on the nights before or after your wedding, that's an issue, if not for you, then for your out-of-town guests. As a considerate host, you should ensure your hotel can accommodate all your plans. A simple inquiry early on becomes more complicated (re: stressful) after rooms get booked.

Sleeping in the hotel lobby shouldn't be part of the plan, although it may still happen anyway.

Where's the (after-)party at?

If you haven't given much thought to an after-party, I suggest it at least becomes part of the conversation. While plenty of your guests will be content to call it a night when the lights flick on, a bunch will not, and in all likelihood, you won't either. This leads to some awkward standing (or stumbling) around in the parking lot while the fervent party animals scope out the next scene.

Hosting some type of after-party allows for a more natural and relaxed transition as people trickle out. Trust me, I understand the last thing you want to do is plan *another* party for even *more* money. However, it's money well spent, and it need not be elaborate. Renting out a room at a nearby restaurant with some modest drunk-friendly snacks and a cash bar is more than enough. The important consideration here is the space for everyone to stay together and continue the revelry. You don't need upscale cuisine and *another* open bar.

PART VI
VENDORS AND FEEDING FRENZIES

"I'm the lyrical vendor, hip-hop is my shop"

—Lil Wayne, rapper

PHOTOGRAPHY AND PAPARAZZI (PART I)

Even though we created a wedding website and posted on social media, I was slightly disappointed when the only photographer who showed up was the one we hired while the paparazzi were noticeably missing. I had already worked out how I would subtly pose for my entrance while making it seem like a candid shot. All for naught. Next time, I guess.

Remember, your photographer has the critical job of providing tangible proof that not only did you survive wedding planning; you also *thrived*. "Thrived," of course, is a subjective term. Sure, they'll photograph your wedding, too, but let's not forget about the essentials here. When this is all over, you'll crave a trophy for your efforts, and it will come in the form of well-crafted wedding photographs (and a wedding ring).

Because the best photographers get booked well in advance, your photographer will probably be one of the first vendors you book after your venue. I know you undoubtedly have a keen eye by virtue of you holding a copy of my book. Based on this perception, I also know you saw in the chapter title that this is merely part one of wedding photography, which will focus on selecting a photographer. The sequel imparts wisdom for photography on your wedding day, and you can find it in the final chapter.

THE GOLD STANDARD

The standard to which you hold your prospective wedding photographer should be higher than that of your other vendors. This is for one simple but fitting purpose: you will spend most of your wedding day with this soul. Liking their personality is critical, and not wanting to shove letter openers in your ears when they talk should be the bare minimum. If you don't get the warm-and-fuzzies when meeting them in the wild, how are they possibly going to ease your wedding-day stress? Your photographer will help manage the flow of events and will be your confidant in the nervous moments leading up to your ceremony.

If you don't already have a personal relationship with your photographer, I highly recommend developing one before your wedding. Take them out for a drink. Ask about their dog. Nothing will put stress to the sword quite like knowing you have an experienced wedding ally to help you loosen up when you're maniacal.

While the first point appeals to your sanity, this next one will appeal to your logic. Your photographer will furnish tangible memories for posterity. If your flowers were devastatingly crimson instead of burgundy, or the DJ accidentally played a song on your do-not-play list (probably "Happy" by Pharrell), these mistakes end when your night ends. Wedding photos will stay with you, presumably, forever. Over time, these photographs will slowly transform from capturing your wedding memories to evoking your wedding memories and finally *becoming* your wedding memories.

Photo advice from the future!

Both for the sake of stress reduction and posterity, my fervent advice is not to skimp on your photographer. If necessary, try to curtail other budgetary items to free up funds for a skilled photographer (hint: flowers and décor are excellent places to start). This is one of the times when both near-future you and old-person you will thank current you.

TRADITIONAL-STYLE PHOTOGRAPHY

Besides personability and professionalism, you are going to, of course, need to admire the photographer's style. We're talking photography style here; their spiked hair with cerulean hues is of no concern to us. For the uninitiated, the premise of style is that different photographers can capture the same event in starkly different ways.

Some photographers specialize in the *classic* or *traditional* approach, which probably adorns your parents' wedding album. This method features posed and staged photos. The photographer directs you on where to stand, where to look, and what to do with your hands (I never know). If you have a mental list of desired photo poses with combinations of people, this is your approach. This is also your preferred option if you're risk averse and want more control over the shots.

PHOTOJOURNALISTIC-STYLE PHOTOGRAPHY

A fresh and ever-popular approach focuses on candid shots and capturing raw emotion. This is known as *photojournalistic* or *documentary* photography. In this style, you'll have less interaction with your photographer, and they will instead operate in the background (or the shadows, as I like to say). You might see them scurrying to capture flawless shots of your guests making fools of themselves or the rare, secluded moments of you with your new spouse.

Expect little posing, if any. Spontaneity is the word here, and this genre seeks to capture your wedding as you live it, not the way your photographer stages it. However, embracing the unexpected involves the potential for awkward photos with unflattering poses. To account for this, expect your photographer to amass an arsenal of diverse shots throughout the night to ensure enough hit the mark.

Despite all the flashing (not the fun kind), you might not get photos with every desired friend and relative because of the impromptu nature of this style. More on how to combat this dilemma later.

SUBCATEGORIES AND MIXED STYLES

Falling under these two dueling styles are more nuanced approaches. I've come across *dramatic, natural, fashion, artistic, stylish*, and even *fine art*, to name a few. Confused? Me too. It seems like photographers are just opening a thesaurus and picking adjectives at this point. Heck, if I manage to snag a picture of one of my cats yawning, it immediately becomes my dramatic capture. These various styles focus on the post-production work undertaken by your photographer.

As a surprise to no one, there's not a dictionary definition of any style. To simplify your quest to discover which photography adjective is ideal for your wedding, determine first whether you prefer posed or unexpected shots—the big differentiator. After that, browse the pictures of your prospective photographers to see which style resonates with you.

They might call it dramatic or artistic. Nomenclature is meaningless; you will see what you like.

Yes, it's possible to seek a mix of both styles—I'm glad you asked. While photographers often specialize, they are professionals and scarcely one-trick ponies. Keep your expectations in check, however. The same way you wouldn't call a real estate lawyer after you get arrested for impersonating a police officer (again), don't expect a classic photographer to snap the same spectacular candids as a documentary photographer. Rank your preference and prioritize accordingly.

Because pictures are blatantly absent from this book, all I can responsibly do is send you away to discover your style. At the risk of being creepy, start saving the wedding photos that sing to you, whether they come from acquaintances or Internet strangers. After several, it should be clear where your preferences lie, and this realization will inform your search.

Prioritize your style.

Jen learned her preferred style by stalking wedding photos posted by her friends and strangers on Pinterest (pinterest.com). She strongly favored the photojournalistic approach while my strong preference was to have a photographer. However, we both still wanted several posed photos with our families. We had an abundance of faith in our photographer to take straightforward staged photos to supplement the candid masterpieces that earned her the job.

Although a classic photographer may have produced more artistic posed photographs, this wasn't the priority for us. All we needed were some point-and-shoot combinations, and she was more than qualified. As we expected, she succeeded magnificently and checked off our "shot list." She even accomplished this feat while suitably instructing me on what I should do with my hands, much to the relief of everyone.

ASSESSING LIKABILITY

Even the best judges of character will find it tough assessing a photographer's personability through a website. Therefore, establish your style first and then select based on personality and price. Speak to the subjects of your photo-stalking and ask about their photographers. While it's easy to skim photos and critique the finished product, you get the inside scoop on personality and pricing through referrals. If there's one thing that photographers love almost as much as their sophisticated cameras, it's referrals. Hashtags too. If you attend any weddings during your search, pay close attention to how the photographer operates.

WHERE TO LOOK

If you don't strike gold with referrals, you'll just have to find a photographer out in the wild—from your couch. As usual, the large commercial websites are a fine starting point. Scour the photos and read the reviews. Glean the photographer's website to see whether it's professional and whether it imparts a good first impression. Warning: ignore red flags like typos and broken pages at your peril. These are professionals who make a living off style and artistic expression. The website should follow suit and is your first indicator of future performance.

~~Two~~ Three peas in a photo pod.

This bears repeating. I really can't overstate how important it is to vibe with your photographer. Accordingly, I heartily suggest meeting your prospective photographers in the flesh. Since personality plays a pivotal role in your decision, you'll want to do your investigation face to face.

Your photographer might be an absolute peach during a phone conversation only for you to learn something unforgivable in person—like a propensity for open-mouth chewing. Or no deodorant. Or those judging eyes (you know what I mean). The list is endless. I've learned to listen to my BS detector during these meetings, and it hasn't steered me wrong yet! Jen may disagree with the caliber of my abilities, but she's not the one writing this.

DIGITAL VS. FILM

While digital photography is prevalent due to the relentless march of technology, some wedding photographers still prefer to incorporate film into their craft. Some might prefer film purely because it's a relic, and weddings are rooted in tradition. Others might just like its quality over digital.

If you're contemplating film, keep a few things in mind. Film tends to be more expensive because of the obvious fees for film processing. Think back to when you used to develop your disposable cameras in the glory days. It wasn't free then, and it isn't cheap now because wedding.

Furthermore, locating studios to develop the negatives isn't always convenient. Even though you will order film prints directly from your photographer, you might need to use this avenue for any negatives you want developed. On that note, ensure you understand whether your photographer will relinquish the negatives so you may develop them on your own.

Digital photography doesn't feature the same film-processing fees. Although it may be cheaper than film, it's not *cheap* because, again, wedding. Unless you're planning to purchase a digital picture frame (more expensive, more practical) or tape an old smartphone to the wall (less expensive, less pragmatic), you will need to print your digital photos.

Your photographer may insist you order prints through them. You might also print your favorites using retail stores and websites. In a similar vein to film negatives, this all depends on who keeps the rights (think copyright) to the digital photos. Sometimes you'll receive the rights, sometimes your photographer will retain them, and sometimes you'll get rights only to the photos of which you order prints. What you're allowed to do with the digital photos should be crystal clear on the contract and in your prospective-photographer discussions.

>
> ### What are you *really* buying here?
>
> Don't breeze past the photo-rights consideration. After your wedding, you'll want to proudly flaunt your wedding conquest to the world. How will you feel when you can't download your photos or use them to farm likes on social media because you don't own the rights? Frustrated? Yeah, that's probably the understatement of the year.
>
> My opinion was simple: I'm paying for the photography, so I want the rights (or at least the ability to download and freely post photos on social media). It seems like a preposterous suggestion otherwise, even when considering wedding lunacy. Remember, photo rights have inherent value, so if you don't receive them for whatever reason, your contract should reflect that with a cheaper bottom line.

PHOTO BOOTHS

Photo booths have become a hugely popular wedding addition because *everyone* loves photo booths, including me, which I know is surprising. Whether enclosed or open-air, photo booths give your guests something else to do other than the traditional wedding trifecta of dancing, eating, and boozing. Usually, the photo booth and boozing dovetail perfectly and the results make for hilarious viewing later. Sometimes your photographer may provide a photo booth setup, or you may have to look to a third party. Your DJ might also do the trick.

If this tickles your fancy, talk to your photographer about options. Even if a photo booth is not within the realm of their offerings, they might have other options like a backdrop and mount for a selfie station. If not, they can at least point you in the right direction or give you some ideas. Check out the Odds and Ends chapter for the DIY photo booth project Jen and I concocted for the same hilarity at a fraction of the cost.

PHOTOGRAPHY IS FOR YOU

I want to impart one last sliver of photographer-related insight. Wedding photography is one of the few components of your wedding that is mainly for *you* as opposed to your guests. As much as your guests will fancy seeing the photos afterward, the photos are for you. They're your memories.

Of all the boundless wedding ingredients that force you to pay through the nose, regard photography as an investment for future you. Couple this with tangible evidence of wedding success, and you should have enough incentive to focus more on quality than cost. You'll be happy you did.

PHOTOGRAPHY CONTRACTS

When it's time to sign your contract, the same overarching pointers in the venue section apply here. Below are some additional questions you should think about before finalizing your photographer / wedding-day sanity protector:

- Do you have our wedding date available? (Le duh)
- Have you ever worked at our venue?
- What exactly is included in each of your packages?
- Do you offer videography? How do those packages work? If not, can you recommend any videographers?
- How many weddings have you shot? How many do you have for this upcoming year?
- How would you describe your photography style?
- Do you charge hourly rates? What is your overtime rate and when does it start?
- Will you do an engagement shoot? Is that included in our package or is it an additional fee?
- Do you shoot both digital and film?
- Do you charge extra fees for traveling to our venue?

- Who will be our actual photographer? Are there substitutes available for emergencies?
- What type of equipment do you use? Do we or the venue have to provide anything?
- Do you offer any extras such as a photo booth or selfie station?
- Who will own the rights to our photos after the wedding? Are there restrictions for sharing these with friends or on social media?
- What type of photo editing will you be doing?
- When can we expect delivery of our photos after the wedding? How does delivery work?
- What is the payment schedule? When is final payment due? What payment methods do you accept? Is there any discount for paying cash?
- What is your cancellation policy?
- *For film*: What are the processing fees?
- *For film*: Do you shoot both in black and white and in color? About what percentage of each?
- *For film*: How does print ordering work? Who owns the negatives?

YES, THEY *ARE* JUST FLOWERS

We both know my feelings on wedding flowers. I think I pick on (the puns are back) flowers so much because they're the best example of the unbelievably inflated costs that rule weddings. Yes, I reluctantly understand you're paying for the flowers, the arrangement, the transportation, the setup, and the takedown. Really, I do. My point is this: even if you were to request the exact same floral elements down to a tee, the price magically increases when the event is a wedding as opposed to, say, an extravagant graduation party. It's a wedding miracle (for the florist).

During wedding planning, I started referring to flowers as "plant genitals" in a brazen act of defiance. I did this to combat my helpless discontent and because I'm mature. Jen was not impressed and rolled her eyes so hard it must have made her dizzy. She recovered. Anyway, there's no point in perpetual frustration, especially after the fact. I just wanted to provide some clarity on why wedding flowers often incur my wrath.

DO YOU HAVE A FLORAL VISION?

Here's an ironic statement coming from me: florists are another essential ally for you and your partner. It's begrudgingly true. Besides providing the flowers, they are often the ones who arrange your centerpieces and put the finishing touches on your decorations before the ceremony and reception. That's one less source of stress on your wedding day.

When shopping around for a florist, it's vital to find a florist whose style matches your vision. For us, it was obviously Jen's vision. Therefore, it's important to *have* a vision. If you're struggling to picture your décor, find some encouragement in magazines and on the Internet, with Pinterest being the fan favorite. Don't call it copying. Call it inspiration! Try to have at least some idea of what you're expecting before meeting with prospective florists, and then let them do the rest.

RIPE FOR COST-CUTTING

Your floral budget is malleable. Simple flower substitutions can have a seemingly disproportionate effect on the final bill. You'd be amazed to see what swapping carnations for hydrangeas will do to your bottom line. Be up front with your florist about cost constraints. They should still be able to match your theme on a budget. Luckily, multiple horticultural combinations exist for each color, even when factoring in the Crayola colors.

Your table centerpieces are the cardinal element of wedding décor—and presumably the most expensive. Besides supplying flowers, your florist might also provide the glassware for both your centerpieces and whatever else you had in mind.

As I alluded to earlier, Jen and I endeavored to make most of our own centerpieces and supplemented these with flowers (see the Odds and Ends chapter for more on this as well as other cost-saving décor ideas). We saved a decent amount of money and learned the ancient art of gluing glass. This is a solid approach to avoid some infamous wedding markup.

Flowers are resilient.

Do flowers die after an hour? No. No, they do not. Repurpose those vibrant plant genitals and save some money along the way! Whether it's reusing the bride's and bridesmaids' bouquets for reception décor or harnessing the ceremony blossoms in your centerpieces, flowers are versatile for everyone. Jen assures me that we did this. I must have been preoccupied with more pressing matters so we're all taking her word for it here. Confer with your venue about the logistics.

Maybe ditch the "flowers" altogether and support the environment along the way? Whether it's fake flowers, paper flowers, or fabric flowers, your creativity (and the creativity of the Internet) is your only limit. If this tickles your fancy, search for "wedding flower substitutes" or "wedding flower alternatives" and prepare to be swamped with ideas. Don't forget to add "eco-friendly" to any of your searches to get Mother Nature's buy-in. You'll certainly find cost-saving (and green) inspiration somewhere in those search results.

Finally, don't forget about buying local. You don't always need a fancy wedding florist to get the job done for your wedding. There are flowers aplenty at local markets, warehouses, and grocery stores, and many will allow you to place orders far in advance, often for a fraction of the cost of a standalone florist.

An extra pair of thumbs. The green ones.

If you decide to DIY your flowers or buy them locally, you will need someone to put everything together, transport it to the venue, and set it up. You will *not* want to deal with this stress on your wedding day. Friends, family, or your wedding party might be able to help, but not always.

Sometimes, just thinking about all that work is enough to justify dropping the extra cash on a professional—or at least an extra set of hands. What you're *really* paying for is stress reduction, forever a savvy investment.

FLORAL CONTRACTS

Your floral contract should include details on the types of flowers, the composition of each bouquet and centerpiece, other centerpiece components, the setup time, the takedown, and all other décor components. In other words, it should be robust. Here is the actual description of Jen's bouquet from our florist contract: "5 playa blanca roses, 3 sahara roses, 3 burgundy roses, 4 burgundy ranunculus, astrantia, eucalyptus, 3 burgundy spray roses, white wax flower, with a no-show lemon leaf collar and a light ivory satin wrap for a handheld."

This is a foreign language to me, but Jen is fluent in overpriced hocus-pocus and that's what mattered. My boutonniere was more my speed: "playa blanca rose boutonniere, $14." That's fancy speak for "I had a white rose pinned to my chest and it was the cheapest part of our wedding." This is the level of detail you're looking for. If applicable, the flowers provided for the ceremony, maid of honor, best man, and cake should also be listed as separate line items.

If your ceremony is in a house of worship, don't forget to check whether there are flower restrictions. There might also be rules on where you can place flowers within the space. Ideally, you want to know this before you meet with your florist so you can cement the logistics.

Being likable is important, both as a member of humanity and when negotiating a contract with your florist. Although you might not even notice your florist on your wedding day, you'll have a fair amount of back-and-forth communication in the weeks leading up to your wedding. You're more likely to get a better deal if your florist wants to work with you as opposed to your florist secretly hoping you take your tantrums elsewhere.

WHAT TO ASK

When vetting potential florists, a worthy first question is whether they have worked with your venue before. While an answer in the affirmative is preferable, a no here isn't necessarily a deal breaker. It means, however, you will want your florist to complete some type of walkthrough at your venue so they can plan accordingly. Your picturesque description and the venue's edited website photos probably won't be sufficient for your florist to... flower.

While it's not uncommon for your florist to handle more than one wedding on any particular date, still try to connect early to ensure they have the bandwidth to deliver for you (both literally and figuratively). In addition to confirming your wedding date is doable, here are a few florist-specific questions to keep in mind:

- How many times have you worked with our venue?
- If unfamiliar with our venue, do you agree to do a walkthrough? Is there a charge for this?
- How many other weddings are you working on our wedding weekend? Do you expect any complications with staffing?
- What flowers will be in season for our wedding? How will these work into our color theme?
- What other décor do you provide besides ~~plant genitals~~ flowers? Is this a rental arrangement or do we have to purchase it?

- Based on our floral selections, what type of lighting do you recommend?
- Will you be doing delivery, setup, and takedown? What are the charges for each of these?
- If we bring our own centerpiece items, will you set these up with our flowers? Is there an extra charge for this?
- Can you provide flowers for the cake? Can you also arrange them on the cake?
- Where can we see the samples of your work?
- Do you have insurance?
- What is the payment schedule? When is the final payment due? Is there any discount for paying cash?
- What is the cancellation policy?

BEATS

I used to play the trumpet in middle school and freshman year of high school. I really loved it and played in the marching band for football games. I was also the epitome of cool. I distinctly remember researching potential careers for trumpet players at one point, which is wholly unsurprising given my propensity for thinking ahead. The result that stuck with me was playing in a wedding band. Career sorted, until of course the debut of the *Fast & Furious* series.

After discussing photography and plant genitals (maybe the title of this book's film adaptation), the last piece to the core-wedding-vendor trifecta is music. Even though the premise is bewildering to me, people love to dance. I was never much of a dancer, but relationships are about compromise and Jen loves to boogie. Aided by a blood-alcohol content that precludes me from driving, I can usually be a worthy partner, if the music is right.

Selecting the right jams is paramount because it sets the tone (now music puns) for your entire wedding. It leads to guests either tearing up the dance floor or moping awkwardly at the dinner tables. The music defines a memorable experience. The quest for that experience begins with your decision for a DJ or a band.

WEDDING BANDS

A quality wedding band is classy—like 1920s gangster-scene classy. The key word, though, is "quality." While rolling out the red carpet for a herd of amateurs may appeal to your budget, their bumbling renditions won't appeal to your ears.

I'm all for giving people a chance, but perhaps not at the most significant event I'll ever plan. Maybe wait for a birthday party or graduation party to blood the new kids. Stick to the seasoned veterans who are adept at weddings. With a professional band, you're signing up for presence throughout the night. They'll actively summon your guests to the dance floor, not just by pleading but by doing!

As expected, high-caliber bands are always more expensive than DJs. There are more members to the ensemble, so it makes sense. Also, even though properly DJ'ing requires a certain level of skill and experience (I'm talking professionals, not your cousin's neighbor with a MacBook), it pales in comparison to the finesse required to be a talented musician. You'll pay a premium for this talent. Like the other vendors, the best bands will get booked quickly. Book as early as you can once you've found the one.

Besides paying more up front, you must also account for the voracious appetite of musicians. Thankfully, they won't go hungry because they have you. It's *so* kind of you to pay for their vendor plates so they can chow down. Work these added costs into your overall calculation on your spreadsheet. Don't forget about tipping each musician!

Weighing heavily into the DJ versus band conundrum is your guest list. Are most of your guests from the same generation or will you have partiers dying to get down to Buddy Holly and Beyoncé in equal measure? Can your band handle the differences in taste? It's important to match your band's primary genre to the music you're largely expecting at your wedding. At the bare minimum, your guests should recognize most of the artists the band can cover.

DJS

DJs have come a long way from the goofy dudes who adorned ill-fitting suits and always, always wore sunglasses inside. Nowadays, DJs are a more professional outfit and most sport innovative equipment. DJs rarely work solo. While they're busy spinning their rhymes to keep your guests jovial, they rely on the master of ceremony (MC) to run the show.

Are you looking for some extra pizazz like custom lighting displays, eye-catching DJ booth themes, or electronic picture montages? You name it. If you're paying for it (you are), they can likely provide it. Some will even offer photo booths and ceremony musicians. How about a Frank Sinatra impersonator belting out songs during dinner? Yes, that's a thing. DJs make a hefty portion of their revenue by upselling these add-ons, so there are options aplenty.

When prospective DJs lay down their best sales pitch, it's easy to picture what they're painting. In a cloud of reverie, you imagine your entrance into your reception: your name constructed in lights, a gentle mist rolling over the floor, and your exuberant guests screaming louder than those at a Taylor Swift concert. It feels good to be you.

Before getting too carried away on the arms of the pseudo-Swifties, remember that your verdict on a DJ should foremost revolve around music. Besides all the technological goodies, DJs have the vital duty of controlling the room during your reception. They know the songs that will get people out of their seats and can easily change the mood with the push of a button. In addition, they can readily blend songs so there is no natural stoppage for your guests to question whether they should take a dancing break. That's right—they will capture your guests. Forever. Or at least until dinner.

The inside-sunglasses bros still exist, however, so make sure you're booking a professional, wedding-caliber DJ. While the DJ who spun your eighth-grade winter dance seemed like a badass at the time, you've since matured (at least marginally). Use that wisdom to book a wedding-suitable DJ. Make sure you find reviews from third-party websites that *explicitly* mention weddings.

Battle of the beats.

I'll walk you through the decision-making process Jen and I underwent because I trust you'll find some of our rationale compelling. The first concern, as I'm sure you can surmise, was the cost. Although bands were more expensive, they were not cost-prohibitive for us. This was mainly because music was high on our priority list. DJs still easily won this battle.

Next, we envisioned our reception music. Although we like *some* of the same music, we also have very, very different tastes. This is probably a result of Jen's love for dancing compared to my occasional tolerance of it. Jen loves "trap" music when it comes to tearing up the dance floor. For the uninitiated, trap is a sub-genre of hip-hop. Here's the only salient tidbit: if Grandma could understand what was being said in trap music, she would be mortified. I prefer the same music my friends and I used to rock out to in high school. My music taste, like my maturity, peaked a long time ago.

Because we wanted the night to showcase both our musical tastes, a DJ seemed like the better option, if not the only option. Perhaps there's a wedding band that can throw down classic rock, newer punk rock, and raunchy hip-hop featuring multiple rappers. We didn't find that unicorn, but if you do, drop me a line; I'm sure I'll need them in the future.

Last, there are specific songs by obscure bands that are dear to us. Instead of asking a band to learn a ton of new songs (which I'm sure would have added to the cost), we went for the DJ, so all these songs were available instantly.

MUSIC IS MORE THAN JUST THE RECEPTION

With so much emphasis placed on the wedding reception, it's easy to overlook your need for ceremony and cocktail-hour tunes. If you're booking a band, you can request a few band members perform during these times for a per-musician fee.

Although this approach probably features a more attractive up-front cost, it will be a challenge to have the musicians scampering back and forth between rooms to set up. If they are performing for the recessional (the music that ends the ceremony), how will they be able to play at cocktail hour only a few minutes later? To eliminate this logistical ordeal, it might make sense to hire more of the band to cover your various pre-reception melodies. Hiring separate musicians—think violinists, cellists, flutists, etc.—also works here.

Symphony No. 9 in DJ minor.

If you and your fiancé cannot settle on your music selection, a compromise might be in the cards. We love compromises because they empower, generate goodwill, and lower the stress that comes from dissonance with your partner. One possibility is to supplement the DJ with a small ensemble for the ceremony and/or cocktail hour. Examples include a pianist and a violinist, a small a cappella group, or a cabaret singer. This will grant you some classical flair without going bankrupt from a full band. And the best part? There's still room for your beloved hip-hop to thunder from a DJ's speakers during the reception.

With the aid of technology, DJs can effortlessly attend to your ceremony, cocktail hour, and reception. They can set up speakers in various locations with preset playlists that start on command. This allows the DJs to kick off your cocktail hour music remotely while they dismantle the ceremony equipment. The same logistical sorcery works for your reception. Make sure you discuss these arrangements before signing any contracts.

Please don't pass the mic.

Remember the wedding fail videos? Craving a surefire way to feature on that playlist? Permit your DJ or band to allow *any* of your guests control of the microphone, even if only for a moment. You would think most professionals already understand this, but if they did, the fail videos wouldn't exist. Want the possibility of a spontaneous marriage proposal smack in the middle of your reception? Go ahead and pass the mic...

WHERE TO LOOK

As predictable as ever, the usual suspects are a fine place to commence the hunt for music: again, commercial wedding websites such as theknot.com, your venue, other vendors, wedding blogs, and friends who have recently gotten married (with wonderful music). In addition to the tried and true, there are also a couple of debutant resources in this section.

Do you often stumble into your apartment at 4:00 a.m. after a night of clubbing and questionable decisions? You may be just the person you need! Your favorite nightclubs all feature pulsing beats. Reach out to the managers of these fine establishments for DJ recommendations. It's probably better to do this one over the phone, depending on how questionable your decisions really were. Don't forget to heed the warning about *professional* wedding DJs. Make sure these club DJs also work weddings and won't turn your reception into a drug-induced rave—unless, of course, that's the point.

BYO... music?

I would be remiss if I didn't at least mention the ultra-frugal choice for some and the last resort for others: being your own DJ with a smartphone or laptop. The major benefit to this approach is obviously that it's cost-free, assuming your venue can provide speakers. Otherwise, you'll be renting and setting them up yourself.

The cons are many. First, you have no idea how the room's mood will evolve throughout the night. How can you possibly construct the right playlist beforehand? You might be able to task an ally to make playlist alterations as the reception progresses. Even so, that's a ton of responsibility to thrust onto someone else—especially an amateur. Is it worth the risk?

Also, how confident are you with your equipment? One technology mishap and you're scrambling to find another phone. What about entrances? Are you going to have an MC or are you planning a very informal wedding? Microphone? If you're contemplating this, seriously consider the logistics of the entire day. You can tell my concerns about this approach. This is a book about eviscerating wedding-planning stress, not increasing it.

Similarly, most bands have music agents that represent multiple bands. Search for these in your area to see what's on offer. If you're looking for classical musicians, try contacting a musical college in your area. You might be able to find great talent at a cheaper cost than a full-blown professional. I would do a quick audition, though. You need to make sure you're getting someone near the top of the class and not the guy who only knows Beethoven as the big dog.

When selecting a band, sample video or audio recordings are often the only way to determine their sound and entertainment value. The same usually applies for DJs. Unfortunately, these recordings can be (and often are) edited. Therefore, reviews are critical. Remember to listen to your BS detector for red flags and general jackassery (another future book title).

Thou shalt not play terrible songs.

Must-play lists and do-not-play lists are popular with DJs but can sometimes come into play with bands as well. Think of these lists as gatekeepers to protect you from obnoxious guest requests and to assure your favorite songs will bellow through your reception space. I jokingly told our DJ that if I heard even five seconds of a do-not-play song, he would regret it. I think the poor guy believed me.

Both these lists are crucial. Give your DJ adequate guidance for the songs you love. Talk to them up front about whether they're comfortable with a hefty must-play list. Some DJs may demand a certain degree of artistic license, but Jen and I believed we were entitled to exactly what we wanted to hear. In fact, this was exactly what we were paying for. Decide what works best for you.

Your do-not-play list is arguably more important here. Give this one the attention it deserves so you don't have music stress on your wedding night. I gave our DJ explicit guidance to ridicule any of our guests who called for a song on our do-not-play list, like "Cotton-Eyed Joe," and he enthusiastically agreed. I suggest you do the same.

WHAT TO ASK

Here are some additional band-specific considerations (DJ-specific questions to follow):

- Who exactly will perform at our wedding and what will they be playing? What happens if a band member has an emergency? Are there alternates?

- When were the samples taken and which musicians were featured? Will those performers be the same for our wedding?

- What type of editing was done to the samples? Is there any raw footage?

- What type of equipment will you be using? Will the venue need to supply anything?

- Have you ever played at our venue? What type of electrical setup do you need?

- How long will you be playing?

- How do breaks work? Can members take rotating breaks, or will there be music stoppages?

- Can someone act as the MC? Do they have experience doing this?

- How does the overtime rate work?

- Are you receptive to requested playlists? What about songs that are different from your normal style?

- Can you learn specific songs if you don't already know them? Is there a charge for this?

Now for the DJs:

- Who exactly is the DJ and who is the MC?

- Have both the DJ and the MC worked with our venue?

- How do the must-play and do-not-play lists work?

- Do you need anything from the venue for setup?

- Will you be able to cover music for the ceremony, cocktail hour, and the reception? What is your logistical plan?

- What effects will you be using throughout the night?
- What types of extras do you offer and what is the price for each?
- Can you provide a microphone and speaker to the officiant(s) for the ceremony? Is there an extra charge for this?

Just a reminder that print-friendly question lists are anxiously waiting for you at weddingplanningsucks.com.

EAT IT

I wrote you a haiku. It's called "Weddings." I'm proud of it.

> *Food for all to eat,*
> *Drinks are everyone's treasure,*
> *Less dancing, more nosh.*

Watch out, Frost; there's a new sheriff in town with no poetry training! This sheriff also gets mighty hungry at weddings.

Everyone loves to eat and drink. It's a fact backed by anthropology, probably. Can we really trust ruffians who don't cherish delicious food? Tough to say. A better question is whether these heathens can earn an invitation to your wedding. An even tougher dilemma.

In this section we're going to discuss wedding food. Yes! Finally, *something* to get excited about. We'll talk through considerations for hiring a caterer if you're using an off-site space. Then we'll hit on tips for dinner and cocktail-hour food. Like any acceptable meal, we'll end with dessert. Since food selection is a highly personal and spiritual journey, this section will be brief; you know what's yum.

P.S. I bet you $20 Jen scolds me for writing a poem about wedding food and drinks before ever writing a poem about her.

CATERING AND THE IMPORTANCE OF NOT PLAYING WITH YOUR FOOD

At this point you're an expert in finding vendors. Well done! For caterers specifically, start with your venue. They will have a list of the caterers they normally work with and might even have information packets for each. However, remember the wedding industry thrives on reciprocal back-scratching. These referrals are no different. Be wary of the potential kickbacks and referral payments. I'm not implying that every referral is nefarious; I'm just imploring you to do your own research before blindly embracing a catering referral from your venue.

OFF-SITE CATERING – WHAT TO ASK

Getting your off-site caterer right is crucial because they'll be running most of the show. You need to be able to rely on them. From a stress standpoint, you need to know your guests are in excellent hands so you can focus your wedding-day anxiety elsewhere—like on why your mother-in-law is wearing white. Here are some considerations:

- Have you worked at our venue before?
- What are the different options that you offer, what is included in each option, and how much does each cost?
- What option do you recommend based on our venue?
- Can you provide references? How recent?
- Can you provide sample menus with costs for each?
- What types of diet do you cater to (kosher, vegan, gluten-free, low-sugar, alien, etc.)?
- How many staff will you be providing for our wedding? How are the staff paid (per event vs. hourly)? If hourly, what are the overtime rates?
- How does tipping work?
- How do you handle the rentals for dinnerware? What are our options?

- What will your role be during the wedding? Are you just serving food or are you helping elsewhere?
- How do you handle alcohol?
- Is a tasting included? How much does it cost? What can we taste?
- Is a wedding cake included? If not, is there a separate cake-cutting fee?
- When will the setup take place? Is the setup included in our package? Who must be present to coordinate the setup?
- When will takedown occur?
- What exactly do you need from us or the venue on our wedding day?
- Do you have insurance?
- What is the payment schedule? When is final payment due? Is there any discount for paying cash?
- What is the cancellation policy?

Don't be afraid to ask for references and don't be shy to call said references. If their previous clients had a positive experience, they should be gushing to talk about it. Ask what they weren't happy with. Ask whether there were enough servers. Ask about the quality of the food and whether there was enough of it (including the more expensive items). Try to find a recent wedding client—one who will still be empathetic to the chaos of wedding planning.

"THE" TASTING

There's good news and bad news when it comes to wedding food. The good news? It's bountiful and usually tasty. The bad news? As a future bride or groom, you likely won't eat more than a few bites of the wedding menu you meticulously select. Despite this tragedy, picking a menu is a rare wedding-planning unicorn because it's both enjoyable and (almost) stress-free.

There are a bazillion stupid decisions you can make during wedding planning; they're bounded only by your imagination. Perhaps the stupidest is not finagling your way into doing a tasting. Some caterers and venues will welcome you for tastings. Others seem to guard their grub like a company secret. Even though it's asinine, prepare to pay a few bucks for the luxury of sampling the food you're already paying through the nose for. Weddings, am I right?

Plate it, then rate it.

When you're doing a tasting, snap pictures and take notes. Jen and I found a simple number rating system to be effective. If possible, ask the caterer to prepare the food exactly as they would prepare it for your guests so you can see how appetizing it looks.

This is a marathon, not a sprint. Pace yourselves! Don't find yourself so engorged at the start that you're dreading the latter choices. You're the VIPs today—simply enjoy it.

SELECTING YOUR MENU

Try to consider your cocktail-hour menu and dinner menu in tandem. Think of it as one cohesive banquet. Start with your dinner menu and then work backward to your cocktail-hour hors d'oeuvres. Aim to avoid overloading any type of food. For example, if steak is one of your entrée choices, maybe avoid red meat at your cocktail-hour carving station. Also, are you having a theme to your wedding? If so, introduce some choices to highlight that theme. It's a painless way to tie it all together.

>
> ### Herbivores get hungry, too.
>
> Don't forget about vegetarian options—both for dinner and hors d'oeuvres. Jen is a vegetarian, and we decided that her kind deserved to eat at our wedding, too. To our amazement, we have been to several weddings where the "vegetarian option" comprised just the sides from the meat entrées. Why yes, carrots and mashed potatoes sounds like a lovely meal.
>
> Thoughtfully planned vegetarian options these days can be phenomenal, even for carnivores. We thought it was respectful to have at least one vegetarian choice listed on the menu. This contrasts with the "silent option," where your guests must request an off-the-menu vegetarian meal at the time of ordering. That's your call.

The age-old dinner choice is whether to have a buffet or seated meal. Historically, buffets were *cheaper* (not cheap) because they required less staff. However, as buffets become more extravagant, the discount narrows. I assume you know the difference between a seated dinner and buffet because you're alive. You can ask your caterer for the options and costs.

Choosing a buffet will naturally compress your reception, as it shortens dinner service. Bear that in mind and plan accordingly. If this bothers you, try extending your cocktail hour and pushing dinner later into the evening to make room for more dancing earlier. Another option is a first seated course—like a salad or pasta—with the buffet stations rolling out later. Again, discuss any timing concerns with your caterer or venue. This isn't their first rodeo.

IF YOU POUR IT, THEY WILL COME.

Alcohol. Many people like it. Some people *really* like it. (Looking at you, Wisconsin.) A few don't drink it. No matter *your* views on it, you've now become an expert in guest consideration. Well done! You know that your guests will be stampeding into your wedding with full hearts, empty stomachs, and unquenchable thirsts. Again, our guests are needy, but we don't hold it against them because (1) we're not monsters and (2) we were needy guests once, too.

The conundrum regarding an open bar or, frankly, anything else is a question of cost. Notice how I explicitly didn't say "cash bar"? I generally discourage cash bars because they create both awkward and negative experiences. For example, some folks might not have their wallets on them when they stroll up to the bar because they weren't expecting to pay for drinks. Then what? That embarrassment and frustration will be targeted at you. Furthermore, true cash bars dampen the party. A cluster of guests may decide to take off earlier than expected so as not to spend all their beer money in one place.

Obviously not everyone wants or can afford an open bar. I absolutely get that. Don't fret. You don't *need* a full open bar to create a thoughtful bar scene for your guests. You can try a limited open bar of beer and wine. It's up to you whether you want to omit the liquor—keeping wallets in pockets—or just have it be cash. To spice things up, you might also be able to furnish a signature drink to each of your guests. Your venue can tell you whether that's feasible.

Also, if money is a concern (it usually is), why not shorten the time frame of the open bar? For example, you could fund the brews during your cocktail hour and the first hour of reception and then either switch to a cash bar or beer and wine. You might also be able to provide a cash bar but pre-fund all the drinks up to a certain dollar threshold.

Some need your wedding more than you do.

To determine your ideal bar arrangement, consider the options and do the math based on how boozy your guests are. *Do not underestimate.* Just because half your friends are (shockingly) parents now does *not* mean they won't drink like they're back on campus. They've been dreaming about this night since you sent the save-the-dates. It's circled on their calendars. They booked the babysitter six months in advance just to be safe. They need this. Don't let them down.

If you still conclude a cash bar is the right fit, all the more power to you! This remains *your* wedding and *your* choice. Always. However, you need to do this the right way; communication with your guests is (almost) as important as communication with your partner. Make sure you let them know about the cash bar beforehand. A wedding website is the perfect place for this notification, but verbal advisements also work. Finally, ensure you plop a few signs up at the bar(s) to avoid any awkward misunderstandings. Your guests (and bartenders) will appreciate it.

PLEASE DON'T DROP OUR CAKE, OR AT LEAST WAIT UNTIL AFTER THE PICTURES

Nothing screams wedding like a visually stunning wedding cake that most of your guests will be too plastered to even notice. Don't despair. You'll still get to cut the cake and the pictures will be exquisite. Let me be clear: in the world of wedding stress, stress over wedding cakes should not happen. Please trust me on this one.

Your cake will be wonderful, your guests might eat said cake, and your cake will taste like cake. If you're a dessert aficionado and want to pursue more decadent options, do it! It should be fun. If you find yourself trekking to the ends of the earth to find the most over-the-top, delicious cake, I envy your passion. So long as you're enjoying the journey, you're doing things right.

Your cake can be as elaborate as you desire or your budget allows. There's substantial latitude for prices here, and even the simplest upgrades might demand a premium because wedding. In the age of social media and the perpetual hunt for likes, photogenic cakes are prevalent. Like many aspects of life, I cared more about function over form. Give me the ugliest gâteau in the world, so long as it's delicious.

Silly me forgot this was a wedding, where normal life rules don't apply.

My mantra should have been "give me the fairest cake in all the land—I care not if it tastes like cardboard." Luckily, our baker (and florist) delivered for us. Like the perfect wedding cake, ours tasted decent and looked amazing (i.e., likes galore). Jen gets the plaudits for the cake design; I win the participation trophy for picking complementary flavors.

Pinterest and wedding blogs are your inspiration allies. See if your baker can use your favorites as guidance. Even though much of your wedding cake will go from kitchen to plate and then back to kitchen, try to still appeal to a large audience. For example, Jen and I were considering a carrot cake option since we both worship it. After casually mentioning it to some friends and family, we received tons of carrot-cake hate. It turns out some barbarians have a deep-rooted disdain for carrot cake. Who knew? Instead, we opted for a safer vanilla cake with chocolate mousse filling. Some people loved it, some people tolerated it, but I imagine fewer people hated it.

Wedding cakes are expensive, and you can tell because of the word "wedding." If your wedding package doesn't include a cake, you can always opt for cheaper (but still delicious) alternative desserts. Some cost-effective ideas include cupcakes, small mini-pies, or towers of doughnuts or cookies. You can play with a multitude of flavors here, so it's kind of like choose your own food coma. Reach out to bakers to see what they can whip up and what they recommend for your guest count. Be conservative when calculating quantities in case any of your gluttonous guests is a real-life version of Bruce from *Matilda*.

The most expensive fruit known to mankind.

Jen and I had an absurd challenge to get either our baker, florist, or venue to place fresh fruit on our wedding cake. We didn't expect issues here because, you know, it's putting fruit on top of a cake. The runaround we got was so bonkers it became hilarious. To make a long story short, our florist reluctantly agreed to complete this back-breaking mission for an extra $200 (!) after our baker and venue eschewed any responsibility.

Did the cake look striking? Absolutely. Was the upgraded look worth the stress? Absolutely not. It would have been impressive-looking either way, and our guests would not have known we omitted the fruit. Don't get worked up over cake what-ifs.

MAKING IT OFFICIAL

No matter what, you need some type of officiant to make this whole escapade legal. If you and your partner are saying "I do" in a place of worship, you're covered by a religious leader. Remember, these religious leaders often don't solemnize marriages outside houses of worship. So if you're opting to get married somewhere else, the path gets trickier. Don't worry, we can handle tricky just fine.

A priest and a rabbi walk into a bar…

Besides the stress-reducing features of an on-site ceremony, Jen and I also opted for this approach because we're an interfaith couple. With her being Jewish and me being Roman Catholic, we decided against either a church or a synagogue. Even so, we wanted the ceremony to include both our faiths, so we looked for a rabbi and a priest to be dual officiants. Boy, was that tough. The priests wouldn't even consider it because we were getting married outside a church, and most of the rabbis said no because I wasn't part of the tribe.

Eventually we hired a quirky, progressive rabbi who had no problem marrying us. On the other side, both figuratively and literally, a wonderful Catholic deacon assisted with the ceremony. I think he felt compelled since I'm his (favorite) nephew. If you're an interfaith couple or perhaps a nontraditional couple in any sense of the word, plan for extra time when finding a religious officiant. Don't be discouraged if you get rejected initially, like we did. The progressive leaders are out there; you *will* be able to include elements of your faith if you so choose.

RELIGIOUS LEADERS

With members of the clergy, know that the vetting process is a two-way street. You might get rejected by a religious institution if you don't meet their traditional standards. Also, prepare for an interview that will broach some *very* personal topics. Why yes, you likely *will* be diving into your sexual histories during these interviews. How exciting!

After you get the holy green light, next up is the sometimes-required pre-marriage counseling—yet another reason not to procrastinate. Not only do you need to make sure your wedding date is available, but every institution's counseling is also a different length. It's usually measured in months, not weeks. Like most ways to reduce stress, the sooner you reach out, the better.

If the institution deems you worthy, you should still ensure this religious leader or congregation is right for you. There may not be much leeway here for the ceremony or the presider. If you're trying to vet styles, the best way to do so is to attend a service where the officiant is presiding.

CIVIL CEREMONIES

While religious ceremonies are foremost about being married in the eyes of God, civil ceremonies focus on marriage under the law. Even though civil ceremonies are obviously more secular, the main difference is simply a legal officiant versus a religious one. However, spirituality can certainly enter the fray in civil rituals if you choose. We already know specific rules govern religious ceremonies. Think of civil ceremonies as anything not conforming to these rules. Welcome aboard.

The options for civil marriage officiants are plentiful. The quickest and easiest way to get married is to drive down to the courthouse and take a number à la the DMV. Unlike the DMV, instead of waiting for two hours only to be told that your birth certificate is a copy and to come back another time, when the courthouse calls your number, you will be married by either a court clerk, judge, or justice of the peace. Keep in mind that some courthouses require appointments. Confirm the specifics *before* you make the trip.

These ceremonies are very secular and formulaic. All the marriage, none of the fuss! Remember, there's no unwritten marriage law precluding you from taking a quick trip to the courthouse and then throwing your reception another day.

Justices of the peace are not confined solely to government buildings; they can solemnize marriages on the road as well. In fact, many have positioned themselves as *another* type of wedding vendor. Some specialize in same-sex or interfaith marriages. This is undoubtedly because they're empathetic to the trouble that many of these couples face when scavenging for an officiant.

With some early research, you should be able to find an officiant who can craft the exact service you're hoping for, no matter your circumstances. By the way, the assumption here is that your officiant can legally perform marriages in your state, but it *always* makes sense to confirm. You know what they say about assumptions...

FRIENDS AND FAMILY

For a personal touch, why not ~~beg~~ ask a close friend or relative to officiate? Trained by the prestigious school of the Internet, nearly anyone over the age of 18 can become an officiant. These pros are sometimes dubbed "civil celebrants." This might be the perfect solution if you desire a very personal ceremony.

Unless you aim to give your BFF free rein over your nuptials, you'll have to do some ceremony planning. What kind of ceremony do you yearn for? Do you want tears or laughs? Both? Don't tell me; tell your officiant! It's *critically* important to be vocal about your preferences so you're not let down at the altar by your officiant. Let your fiancé do that. Kidding, of course.

From a logistical standpoint, involving a best friend or close family member can help balance your wedding party if you have too many bridesmaids or groomsmen. Why not promote your best man or maid of honor to officiant? The hours are an improvement, but the second boss is a drag. Again, laws about these "online officiants" vary down to the *county* level in the United States. It's your job to confirm permissibility. Otherwise, you'll still be making a trip to the courthouse after the fact.

A license to wed is easier than your road test.

Jen is a wedding aficionado, having officiated two weddings before ours. I like to say it was only natural for her to be less stressed about our wedding because it was her third wedding. I got a begrudged smirk at first and perpetual eye rolls thereafter.

Jen's process for getting licensed was criminally easy. She literally signed up on a website, certified she was over 18, paid $40, and then received a wedding kit in the mail, packed with everything from a clergy parking pass (!) to a sample ceremony guide. We never tried the parking pass, but if becoming a ceremonial officiant will help me find NYC parking, sign me up. She did have one or two extra hoops to jump through when she officiated a wedding in New York State, so again, focus on the state-by-state requirements. I think this is the third time I'm saying it.

WHAT TO ASK

As always, I won't throw you to the lions without first prepping you with some questions to consider when vetting officiants. Keep in mind that members of the clergy might perceive asking too many questions as disrespectful. So brevity rules in houses of worship. Here are the considerations:

- How long have you been solemnizing weddings? Are you licensed in our state?
- What is your style for wedding ceremonies? Will you incorporate any religious overtones, or will the ceremony be strictly secular?
- Can we personalize the ceremony script? What input do we have?
- What will the preparation schedule look like in the months leading up to our wedding? What time commitment will we need?
- Do you impose any restrictions (décor, music, photography, dress, etc.)?
- What is the fee and when is payment due?
- Will you be present at the rehearsal? Is there an extra fee for this?
- *For friends and family*: How comfortable are you with public speaking? Are you easily understood? Will you be crying during the entire ceremony? Do you ugly-cry? (Only half kidding on this one.)
- *For friends and family*: How involved will you be in crafting the ceremony? Are you comfortable coming up with a script on your own?

Forget the license, forget the wedding.

Don't forget about the marriage license. As our rabbi only half joked, "No license, no marriage." He then regaled us with a wedding where the couple forgot the license, so he refused to do the ceremony. He did say it ended up working out but never quite told us how. Jen and I got our license the next week. I also checked that we had it packed about 10 times before we left for our venue. There's an expiration on these suckers, so that should dictate when you grab yours.

PART VII
TO YOUR HEAD COUNT, FROM YOUR GUESTS

"Hospitality is about making your guests feel at home, even if you wish they were."

—*Unknown*

At some point during the unbridled psychosis that can only arise from calling far too many vendors, you will remember your guests. "What guests?" Yes, I, too, fell into the trap of forgetting that actual human beings would be attending our wedding. Oops. When Jen sat me down and gently explained that "head count" was not just a costly phrase and each number represented a person, it all made sense.

Your guests are a big deal. Not only are they most of your favorite creatures, but without them, you wouldn't be renting out a massive venue space, wouldn't need music, wouldn't need flowers, wouldn't need a bar, wouldn't need an elaborate dinner, etc. When we say it like that, our guests are needy.

This part will run through the basics of turning your head count into guests by inviting them to your wedding. The fabled wedding spreadsheet will make an appearance, so if you haven't read the budgeting chapter, you might consider giving it a glance before reading on.

Now then, let's get to it. A limited head count, multiple parties with dueling interests, budgetary constraints, exiled family members—what could possibly go wrong?

SAVE-THE-DATES

Naturally, you're going to imbue a ton of importance onto your wedding. Duh. It's *your* wedding. You know whose wedding it's not? Your guests' wedding. Inevitably, some invitees may not attend for a host of legitimate or bootleg reasons. The first step to crafting your final guest list is to send save-the-dates (the fun STDs) and hear informally about who has conflicts. The lucky folks who receive the save-the-date should notify you of issues before you even send invitations. Don't count on that courtesy, however.

The consensus for when to send save-the-dates is anywhere from 6 to 12 months before your wedding. Eight months is most popular. If you're planning a destination wedding or have a significant cohort of out-of-town guests, you might want to send them on the earlier side of that range. If you prefer to wait, it's a good idea to give advanced notice to future invitees whose method of transportation will start with a plane.

You don't want them to curse your procrastination as the reason they missed out on all the good flight deals.

Save-the-dates are, by nature, announcements. You're proclaiming your marriage to your guests! Hallelujah! You're also touting the end of wedding planning, but no one else seems to care about that. Save-the-dates are *not* invitations, so don't feel compelled to make them fancy. Postcards are fine, and magnets are another popular choice. There are only a few requirements: your names, your wedding date (including year), and the city. Pictures are optional, but I recommend including one to avoid any embarrassing confusion from your guests.

You've been keeping a running list of guest addresses in your spreadsheet, right? No? Well, no time like the present! Maintaining guest contact information from the outset of planning is a fantastic way to avoid a scramble later. Don't forget to keep it updated. Be on the lookout for any of your guests moving and update their addresses accordingly. This is especially important since there's often a large chunk of time between when you mail your save-the-dates and when you mail your invitations.

Your handwriting (possibly) sucks.

Scores of wedding-stationery websites also offer envelope printing, either "free" with your purchase or for a nominal fee. This is yet another perk of tracking addresses with a spreadsheet. It might take some effort to input the addresses from your spreadsheet into the format these websites require. However, compared to writing them out yourself, you'll save oodles of time.

The die-hard traditionalists may scoff at printed addresses in lieu of handwritten calligraphy. Thankfully, we're not in that faction of snobs; we're just trying to make this as painless as possible. The pursuit of immaculate penmanship is stressful and time-consuming. Go for the printed addresses on all your stationery—it's absolutely worth the cost.

WEDDING WEBSITES

Custom wedding websites are a fun and useful tool in your wedding-planning arsenal. You can set them up for free with no technological wizardry necessary. Want to keep your save-the-dates and invitations clean? Just drop a website link on your save-the-dates and point your guests there for details like accommodations and gift registries. Nice.

In case it's not obvious or you're several drinks in, this means you should set up your website *before* ordering save-the-dates. A few places to build your custom website include our usual suspects—theknot.com, weddingwire.com, minted.com, and zola.com. Remember, there's no such thing as a free lunch. Even though many wedding websites are free in that they don't steal your money, expect copious advertisements. One perk, however, is that some of these sites offer discounts on stationery when you create your website with them. Have a look around and see what you like.

GUEST COUNT: GUESTS COUNT

Labeling the crafting of your guest list as "stressful" is like calling the Great Depression a tough time. Okay, maybe not quite that bad, but I'm dramatic, remember? It's still an understatement. It's *not* too dramatic to say that guest-list decisions can have lasting impacts on family dynamics—far outliving your wedding day. I outlined some points below to help shepherd you through this process as painlessly as possible. A couple of these might sound familiar:

- **Stay on the same team.** If you remember way back to our chat during the communication section, this was the mantra I said you should try to follow, and here we are. With multiple stakeholders in this exercise, it's critical to recall that you and your partner are the VIPs and should try to stick together as much as possible. If there's ever a significant disagreement between you or your partner and any third party, the rule of thumb is to stick with your companion. It's far more gratifying to team up with your fiancé to face the world than tackle an internal rift that will fracture the planning process. It's easier, too.

- **Pick your battles and compromise.** Maybe you prefer that your partner's obnoxious attention-hungry "friend" is excluded from the festivities. If this would devastate your partner or lead to considerable and prolonged drama, add them to the guest list and don't look back. Minor peeves don't take priority over meaningful requests. On the same note, communicate with your partner if there are one or two such people your partner initially dismisses. Compromise means both your voices are heard. Solve problems in good faith; entering the realm of vindictive quid pro quo will help no one.

- **Money talks.** Don't forget about the implicit IOU you signed when accepting those family donations. It's time to pay the piper, whoever that is. Be prepared to entertain at least *some* third-party requests. Before you get *too* bummed, remember, the older revelers will probably give more generous gifts. Consider this point before you nix Dad's golf buddies. However, if these invites become excessive, there's nothing wrong with asking Mom and Dad to tone it down.

- **Don't forget about the B-list.** Sometimes, the best way to smooth over a heated disagreement is to "kind of" invite someone. I'm talking about the iconic B-list. For the uninformed, it's exactly what it sounds like. As you get your RSVPs and discover that your venue and budget can accommodate more guests, you send out invitations to your B-list. Jen and I found this helpful when on the fence about certain people or as a compromise. See the invitation section for how to tactfully accomplish this.

- **Stay consistent with kids and single guests.** Devise a plan for how you will handle kids and plus-ones. Then stick to it. When one of your guests inevitably complains about her child (who happens to be God's greatest gift to mankind) not getting an invite, you can simply reply that you're not inviting kids. Jen and I have a few young cousins we wished to include. However, we also didn't want to turn our wedding into a daycare. We ruled that for youngsters, it would be family only. We gave out-of-town guests a plus-one but omitted plus-ones for the locals who were not in long-term relationships. Just shoot for consistency.

Please don't come to our wedding. Just kidding, kind of. Haha…

On *average*, you can expect about 75–85% of your invitees to show up on game day. That's not an exact science so don't treat it as such. If everyone attending—or even 90%—will destroy your budget, you're going to have a bad time. You don't want to be anxiously checking the RSVPs for declinations so you can afford your wedding. If you have stress about your budget (we all do), be more conservative with the guest count and save for 85% to 90% attendance. Anything lower is just a bonus—financially, of course.

INVITATIONS

Drop these in the mail six to eight weeks before your wedding date. I know that was your question. This isn't *my* answer; it's *tradition's* answer. However, the rise of the B-list modernizes that tradition, and the timeline often gets pushed much earlier. I'll explain the timing details shortly so you can decide how much procrastination is right for you.

Anyone who received a save-the-date should also get an invitation. Period. Yes, mail it along even if they told you they can't make it. Save-the-date chatter is informal; invitations are formal. Besides, if someone RSVPs no and shows up anyway, you'll have written proof for why you kicked them out. Probably just a joke, but you never really know, do you?

A B-LIST FOR A-PAINLESS GUEST LIST

Occasionally the B-list will get a bad rap, but that's due to a complete fumbling of its proper execution. Don't fear it; embrace it. With the proper implementation, it's a helpful tool in quelling guest-list disputes and lowering stress. Here's the secret sauce:

- **Start early.** If your initial foray into B-list consideration is when you're ready to send invitations, it's already too late. Discuss it early with your partner and come up with a mutually agreeable plan for who is on your B-list. Rank this list.

- **Order separate RSVP cards.** This is sometimes overlooked. Since you are sending out B-list invitations later than your main invitations (sometimes called your A-list), the B-list RSVP date should be later than the A-list RSVP date. When determining dates, work backward. Set your B-list RSVP date for three to four weeks before your wedding and then set your A-list RSVP date for around five weeks before that. I recognize this may be confusing; the sample timelines at the end of these points will provide clarity.

- **Order blank envelopes.** Assuming you opt for the pre-printed invitation envelopes, make sure you order several extra invitations with blank envelopes. This is true even if you include your entire B-list on the pre-prints. Guest-list changes are commonplace. You might find yourself needing to (neatly) write out several addresses. Not a big deal at all if you have extras.

- **Send each set of invitations together.** Except for some funky one-offs, strive to only send out invitations twice—once to your full A-list and once to any of the B-list folks who made the cut. Ideally, you want to give your guests three to four weeks to RSVP. Once the A-list RSVPs come back, you will need to quickly determine how many on your B-list will get invites. This is why ranking is important.

- **Try to keep groups on the same list.** We've already established that people *love* wedding gossip. Even though the B-list is one of the worst-kept secrets of wedding planning, you still want to maintain some semblance of secrecy when putting the B-list into practice. If two friends receive invitations at different times with different RSVP dates, your B-list will be evident. Either demote the A-lister or promote the B-lister.

Here are two examples to clarify—one with a B-list and one without. We'll assume a November 15 wedding date for both and work backward.

Example 1: Traditional Schedule

Wedding Date	November 15
RSVP Date	October 15
Invitations Mailed	September 15

Example 2: B-List Schedule

Wedding Date	November 15
RSVP Date (B-List)	October 25
Invitations Mailed (B-List)	September 25
RSVP Date (A-List)	September 18
Invitations Mailed (A-List)	August 18

As you can see, implementing a B-list will push your A-list mailing earlier. These schedules are just guidelines for illustration; don't take them as gospel. They are simply meant to help you plan your timeline to accommodate a B-list if you so choose.

CRAFTING YOUR INVITATIONS

You've received enough wedding invitations to know what goes in them. No? Here's a quick list just in case:

- The invitation (duh)
- The RSVP card with meal choice

- The RSVP envelope
- Reception information/directions
- Lodging information
- Transportation information
- Pre- or post-wedding activities

Some of these points won't be applicable to everyone. Remember, you can point folks to your wedding website instead of covering the universe in your paper invitations. This is a personal choice based on how formal you want your invitations.

Stamp out the stupid.

Jen struck up a wedding conversation with her kickboxing instructor because I guess that's what you do during kickboxing class. Her instructor recently got married and cautioned that she only received RSVPs from about 50% (!) of her invitees. When Jen asked why, her instructor was dumfounded but thought maybe it was because she didn't put stamps on the return envelopes. *Yes, of course that's the reason.* I thought putting stamps on return envelopes was as obvious as not drinking bleach. Apparently not. Please put stamps on your RSVP envelopes. I'm embarrassed I have to say it.

I want to highlight a sometimes-forgotten point: the wedding dress code. *You need to explicitly state it on the invitation.* An omission means you're leaving the choice up to your guests. Bold move. If you're expecting tuxedos but instead get khakis, brown sneakers, and white socks, don't blame your guests for a lack of direction.

Invitation tips and tricks (adopt a dog).

The act of stuffing your invitation envelopes is inherently easy. It's so simple, in fact, that Jen didn't even have to perform her usual quality control on the ones I put together. I am able and I am strong. We picked up a few tricks to make the process even easier and avoid unnecessary hassles later:

- **Use invisible ink.** This is a fun one. Inevitably, at least one absent-minded couple will be too distracted with life to write their names on the RSVP card. Instead of channeling your inner sleuth by analyzing handwriting, just invest less than $10 in a couple of invisible ink pens with black lights. As you pack the RSVP cards into the invitations, write a small number on the back of each RSVP card in invisible ink. Track which number corresponds to what invitation on your spreadsheet. When you receive a blank RSVP card, all it takes is a quick shine of the black light to see which of your guests had better things to do than follow directions.

- **Weigh a full invitation at the post office.** Letters heavier than one ounce require extra postage, at least in the United States. With fancy invitation paper and all the inclusions, surpassing one ounce is easier than you think. Jen and I made the one-stamp cutoff, albeit just barely. That confirmation from the post office gave us both some much-needed peace of mind. The alternative, of course, is to just wing it. It's not like your invitations will get returned for inadequate postage one month later, right?

- **Invest in an envelope wetter.** The obvious first choice here is a dog who can lick your envelopes for you. For those of us not currently blessed with a canine best friend, invest in a refillable envelope wetter to save you time, energy, and horrendous paper cuts on your tongue. It's probably the best $3 you can spend at this point in your life.

NAVIGATING THE WEDDING REGISTRY

I'm not big into gifts. Both my mother and Jen curse my indifference for material items when buying me presents. As such, I found our wedding registry to be an audacious venture—far out of my comfort zone. I well know this is a *me* problem. Many of you are looking forward to this and will find the repetitive scanning of future gifts to be invigorating rather than awkward. Be warned: the process can be overwhelming, regardless of your fondness for gifts. Jen loves presents, and she agrees.

Try to register with stores on the earlier side (what a shocker). This is especially important if you're having a bridal shower. Also, if you list your wedding website on your save-the-dates, your guests will expect to find your registry on that website. Make it happen.

When registry selection is nigh, you might grapple with the same question Jen and I considered: should we be choosing items we can use immediately, or should we be selecting with an eye to the future? China is an outstanding example. Sure, *someday* we'll want china. It will probably be when I start tucking in my T-shirts and sporting long socks. Right now, however, we're solely focused on surviving NYC and enjoying what's left of our lives before the real adulting responsibilities, like kids and colonoscopies—whatever those are.

> **Don't worry, I'm sure your guests know *exactly* what you want.**
>
> For whatever reason, some couples opt to forgo the registry altogether. Perhaps they hope to be adorned only with cash. Maybe these kind souls are too humble to request their guests make purchases on their behalf. All we can do is speculate. If you abstain from setting up a registry, your guests will also speculate, and their conclusion might not match your intentions. In this case, prepare for guests to gift you whatever they want, for better or worse. It's also an unwritten rule that gift receipts rarely accompany terrible gifts. Enjoy!

We opted for a more practical registry and generally sought items we could use right away, with only a few future luxuries. Your answer to this question will depend on how easily you can store boxes and how badly you need (or want) new staples like kitchenware and bedding. There is no single right answer, and it's only a registry, so don't overthink it.

There are only a handful of additional nuggets of learned wisdom from me this time:

- **Keep an eye out for registry perks.** Many retail stores will entice you to register with them by offering bonuses, such as free gifts when your guests buy a certain number of branded items from your registry. These are known as "completion bonuses." Some stores also give you a gift card based on your guests' total registry spending. Shop around before committing so you don't miss out on these neat perks.

- **Don't register for expensive appliances unless you're ready to use them.** The march of technology stops for no one, including you. If you don't anticipate using a small appliance for at least a few months, it's best to keep it off your registry and use some of your gifted cash to buy it when you're ready. These appliances can become obsolete quicker than you think. Plus, the warranty starts ticking the moment they're purchased, *not* when you finally take them out for a spin.

- **Register for gifts in a wide price range.** Although registering for a $200 robotic garbage can might feel ostentatious, it also makes for a unique one-and-done gift. Cheaper stocking stuffers have utility as add-on presents. However, if you solely cram your registry with them, you'll leave your guests scurrying to buy enough. Include a mix of high-ticket swag and affordable staples. Your guests will appreciate it.

Your spreadsheet never stops loving you.

After your wedding, don't even think about abandoning the spreadsheet that propped you up through the countless throes of planning. How dare you. When you're in post-wedding glory and opening the generous presents from your guests, your ~~best friend~~ spreadsheet should be right next to you, as always, so you can keep track of who gifted you what. This will aid you in your quest to send thoughtful thank-you cards.

PART VIII
ODDS AND ENDS

"Sometimes I really feel like I don't belong here, like I'm supposed to be someplace else."

—Hercules, Disney animation

PART VIII: ODDS AND ENDS

I think I was born without the right side of my brain. I mean, my brain is allegedly a normal shape, but the left side surely commandeered the right, probably because of some disagreement in the womb. As a result of my cranial civil war, logic replaced creativity and science replaced art. Thankfully, Jen's right brain is sophisticated enough for the both of us and made light work of DIY projects for our wedding. This kept our budget on track (appeasing me) and spurred some creative wedding flair (pleasing her). I want to share her successes.

This section is aptly named because it contains a hodgepodge of topics. Expect copious bullet points. Besides the DIY tips I learned from Jen, we'll also cover random wedding additions, wedding favors, and your honeymoon—by far the best part of wedding planning.

ODDS: DECORATIONS, DIY, AND RANDOM ADDITIONS

If you're creative and like to save money, DIY might be for you. If you're not creative but still like to save money, find a creative fiancé. If creativity eludes both of you and you *still* hope to save money, bribe a creative friend or relative. Those are your options.

If you fall into the third bucket, don't fret—the list of artisans willing to help will be surprisingly long. Everyone loves to aid with the décor because it can be fun, is usually relaxing, and doesn't involve the awful parts of wedding planning. These baby projects actually *entice* people to look forward to wedding planning. If only they knew the terrors we've seen. Someday…

Less stress is cash money.

For DIY, you must ask yourself how much your time is worth. Let's take a fancy welcome sign. If you can save $100 by making the sign yourself but it will take eight hours of a Saturday to do so, are you okay working at $12.50 per hour? To be fair, that's more than I made at my first job—but I was also 14. The needle will fall at a unique spot for everyone based on budgets, free time, and stress levels.

Don't forget to consider that your mental well-being has worth, too. This is something I often failed to assess. As a result, I piled on stress for the sake of saving money. Instead of contemplating whether you would work for $12.50 per hour, ask yourself if you would pay $12.50 per hour to lower your stress. Based on the specific trade-off, you might find yourself paying cash for peace of mind. It's a wise investment.

When tackling DIY and decorations, don't discount sourcing used items. Some might scoff at that idea, but don't let your pride impede maximizing your budget. There are myriad wedding-swap groups on social media. Oftentimes, newlyweds use these groups to offload a sea of wedding items (especially décor and centerpieces). These can be a gold mine for stretching your cash without skimping on quality. Craigslist and eBay are other favorites. Have a look—it may surprise you.

Below is an eclectic collection of guidance and war stories from our wedding. If you're more of a visual learner, I'll have some photos of this glory on my website (weddingplanningsucks.com), too. This is the best honest advice I can give you. I hope you find some utility in this alphabet soup:

- **Create your own open-air photo booth.** I love everything about photo booths... except the inflated cost. Since Jen shares my photo booth affection and admires instant film (à la Polaroids), we combined the two to make our own open-air photo booth. We made use of Jen's instant camera and our photographer was nice enough to lend us a tripod and backdrop for no additional charge. If your photographer isn't willing to help (maybe ask why not), these are not big-ticket items to purchase. After securing these key components, add some flair! I'm talking about quintessential photo booth props since everyone wants to wear a paper mustache. Don't forget the copious film and extra batteries!

The only wrinkle with an instant camera is the need for an operator. Our venue supplied a dedicated staff member for a modest fee. If this isn't an option for you, consider enlisting members of your wedding party to keep an eye on things. There's one final necessity: a guest book (see the next point).

An alternate approach is a selfie station where guests use their own phones to take "photo booth" pictures... without the photo booth. You can buy this hardware online. The downside is no physical photos; you'll be relying on your guests to upload these masterpieces to social media.

- **Set up a guest book.** Guest books are ridiculously easy to navigate. Simply buy a scrapbook kit that's chock-full of markers and stickers. Then leave it out at reception and let your guests unleash their creative genius. We had ours right next to our DIY photo booth with instructions for leaving a photo in the book with a message. We also supplied small magnets with glue sticks for anyone who wanted to turn a photo into a souvenir. The whole setup was amazingly cheap, easy to configure, and appreciated by our guests. That's a win.

- **Craft your own centerpieces.** The possibilities are endless, and the inspiration is everywhere. However, I want you to consider a few points before you order 200 nonrefundable mason jars. First, where will you store this stuff? Second, how are you planning to transport everything to your venue? Third, have you discussed arranging the centerpieces with your florist?

    I recommend ordering small quantities to start. You'll need to test the ease of assembly and the display of the final ensemble. What appears fantastic in a magazine might look tacky without a slew of light filters. When scouting for materials, we had extraordinary success at dollar stores, wholesalers, and large craft stores. This was especially true for glassware. It's nearly impossible to beat the end-of-season clearance sales at the large craft stores.

    Our centerpieces were a mix of hurricane vases glued to

tiered long-stem tea light holders, lanterns glued to candlestick holders, several votives, and a smattering of flowers, all arranged by our florist. It sounds strange; however, to my surprise but not Jen's, it looked elegant. All in, it probably cost us around $20 per table for the hardware.

We traded time for money and I still have macabre nightmares about gluing centerpieces. If we purchased this setup from the florist or as finished pieces, the price would have been closer to $75 per table. This is how we justified spending unconscionable amounts of time on assembly.

This last point might be the most important: if you're gluing glass to glass, pick yourself up some clear Gorilla Glue. We became glue connoisseurs from this project (mainly after heaps of broken glass), and this was the only glue that worked every single time while remaining transparent. I highly recommend it.

- **Bathroom toiletries.** Setting up baskets of restroom toiletries shows a touch of class without breaking the bank. Besides, they might come to your rescue throughout the night as well! A few example inclusions for the men's basket are mints, body spray, gum, acetaminophen or ibuprofen, stain-remover pens, Band-Aids, hairspray, a lint brush, acid relief, a comb, and moisturizing lotion. For the ladies' basket, besides *everything* in the men's, Jen tells me to include tampons, bobby pins, safety pins, and clear nail polish (for runs in stockings, allegedly).

- **Make your own card box.** This was my mom's idea. Moms are great. She went ham and built us a gorgeous wooden card holder from scratch. It still sits on display in our apartment. If you're like me and constantly hit your finger when trying to hammer in a nail, fear not—far simpler projects exist. One such project is to buy a white mailbox to paint and personalize as much as you desire. If this type of project doesn't energize you, a variety of these boxes are sold online for under $25. Crisis averted. Easy.

- **Consider flip-flops for the ladies.** The culmination of my life experience has taught me that women love to dance. It has also taught me that for footwear, they value looks above comfort, especially for weddings. A simple way to show your thoughtfulness to the ladies (and their partners they bombast with complaints) is to provide flip-flops for when it's time to ditch the stilettos. I found them in bulk on eBay and paid $1 for each pair. Some dollar stores also carry flip-flops, but they were consistently out of stock when we looked. Don't wait until the last minute, especially near the heat of summer.

- **Don't forget signature drink signs.** We're all creatures of habit. But what better way for your guests to break away from their go-to libations than enticing them with a vibrant new drink on your dime? If you're going the signature drink route, you'll need a way to let your guests know. Don't rely on the bartenders for this.

  You can easily make these signs yourself on the computer and frame them for the bar. If you want to jazz things up, buy a signature drink template from websites like Etsy (etsy.com) for around 10 bucks, complete with drink pictures and fancy fonts. Even *I* could tap into my dilapidated creativity to painlessly craft one such sign.

- **Welcome signs.** Jen made her own using some plywood, paint, and fake flowers to match our color theme. We had it set up on an easel to proclaim our marriage—or at least proclaim to our guests that they were indeed in the right location. We still have it up in our apartment in case we forget we're married.

- **Wedding favors.** Just like the coveted goodie bags from years past, wedding favors are one last way to thank your guests for showing up to the soiree you spent months planning. Perhaps the mighty and versatile mason jar filled with something playful to match your theme? I've also seen bottles of wine adorned with the names of the newlyweds, personalized bottle openers (key bottle openers are wildly popular), and coasters. It's amusing how so many favors revolve around drinking. Anyway, order a bunch more than you think you need.

- **Welcome bags for the out-of-towners.** You'll want to drop these off at your hotel several days before your wedding. Don't forget distribution instructions for the staff. Be sure to drop a note in the bags for any extracurriculars (e.g., morning-after brunch) so your visitors aren't left guessing. Some things you might include are snacks, bottled water, your best remedy for a hangover, and gum/mints/candy. You can easily snag some wedding-themed paper bags online or enclose everything in a tote for a wedding keepsake for your travelers.

ENDS: HONEYMOONING

As we've seen, not *everything* regarding wedding planning is an abomination. If we compare wedding planning to a desert, your honeymoon is a lush oasis. You'll enjoy this. Since this isn't a travel book, you won't find general travel advice here; you're an adult and you know how to pack a suitcase. Instead, I furnish three honeymoon-specific tips as you inch closer to your wedding day:

- **Give yourself an extra day (or two) after your wedding.** Assuming you can swing this with work, you'll be thankful you did. While you're packing your bags to get hitched, you don't want to focus on ensuring your sunscreen and passports make it into your suitcase. You'll want to devote the universe of your mental strength to the pre-wedding fervor. You can ruminate on packing for your honeymoon once you're safely in post-wedding glory.

- **Consider an easy honeymoon with a larger trip later.** Some call it a "mini moon," but don't sell it short—it's a honeymoon. You can always plot a grandiose voyage down the line; the amount of free time you have when not planning a wedding is astounding. For your honeymoon, consider looking into trips that don't require a mountain of planning. Think all-inclusive resorts and flight packages where you reserve everything at once. There's more than enough wedding-planning stress without adding honeymoon stress into the mix.

- **Tell the world.** On your trip, don't be shy about letting anyone and everyone know it's your honeymoon. If you're too shy (or awkward) to pull this off, pick up a couple witty newlywed T-shirts and hope the gatekeepers are observant. You might score some outstanding perks like free champagne, dessert, or an upgraded hotel room or plane fare. Besides copious free food and drinks on our flight, one of our flight attendants took some engagement-esque photos of us in the cockpit on our outbound flight. As cockpit pictures had eluded me while I was growing up, this finally completed me. Thanks, wedding.

Hi, TSA.

By the way, if I *were* going to insult your competence in adulting, I would remind you to check your passport expiration date if traveling abroad. The expiration date needs to be at least six months after your scheduled return. You obviously knew that, though, so I won't remind you.

PART IX
IT'S THE FINAL COUNTDOWN

*"Not to spoil the ending for you,
but everything is going to be okay."*

—*Random wall art you can buy on the Internet*

PART IX: IT'S THE FINAL COUNTDOWN

It's the final countdown! Cue the keyboard riffs and Joey Tempest's ubiquitous vocals. Keep that tune in your head and hum it often, for there is nothing more powerful to carry you across the proverbial finish line. This is it, folks, and on your behalf, I can hardly contain myself.

This section will cover your wedding day. If you were expecting long-winded instructions, prepare to be disappointed; this is just some final parting advice. Please trust me when I say you won't need more than that. You did nearly all the arduous labor. Now it's time to enjoy the fruits of that labor. If you aren't already, try to get yourself amped for what is sure to be one of the best and most memorable days of your life.

VOWS

We kick off this section with vows because you will undoubtedly reflect on them before your wedding day—perhaps a few weeks before, a few days before, or (hopefully not) only a few hours before. Vows are deeply personal. Your major decision is whether to recite traditional religious vows, write your own, or incorporate some combination of both. If your ceremony is in a house of worship, you may not have a choice at all. Check with your officiant.

Traditional vows span generations. There's a reason these hallowed words have stood the test of time, not unlike classical music, Shakespeare, and prenuptial agreements. The content of conventional vows differs for each religion. It's up to you to judge whether these timeless lyrics resonate with you as a couple.

If the traditional approach doesn't begin to describe everything that's in your heart, you may want to pen your own vows. Here are some pointers:

- **Coordinate with your partner.** Establish ground rules about content. While you want your vows to be a surprise to your partner, hashing out a general structure in advance will ensure both your vows are comparable in length and tone. There's nothing cringier than a heartfelt manifesto of passion by one partner only to be succeeded by a punchline-filled 20-second pitch by the other.

- **Enlist the help of a mutual friend.** Send both vows to a trusted confidant and have them verify they are not wildly different in style. This hero should also attempt to ensure neither set of vows is objectively better than the other and neither one of you is going off the deep end. Recruiting a *trusted* friend is paramount here—you need the tough love beforehand to spare yourself the potential embarrassment when you do it live.

- **Don't forget the why.** This stress-reduction tip can also instill often-forgotten clarity when you're drafting your vows. While testing a new standup routine might sound enticing, your ceremony is generally a solemn affair. You're on the verge of pledging a lifetime to your partner. *This* is why you chose to get married. Don't lose sight of it during wedding planning and don't forget it when writing your vows. Humor is effective at easing nerves, and you should use it tastefully; however, your vows should always include the serious devotion to your partner.

- **Practice makes perfect.** Read your vows—again and again. Say them out loud. What sounds fine in your head might sound noticeably awkward when voiced aloud. You should be comfortable enough with your words that you can gaze at your partner when reciting them. If you find the courage (and bountiful spare time) to memorize your vows, keep a written copy in your pocket, just in case. Stage fright is real.

Vow to mix your vows.

If you're on the fence between traditional vows and writing your own, employing a mix might be your solution. Jen and I went this route. We started with a mix of humor and passion in our own vows. After we melted each other's hearts and ran the mascara of family, close friends, and our bridal attendant for some reason, our officiants led us into a medley of traditional Catholic and Jewish vows. For us, this perfectly combined eminent tradition and personalization.

Hire *your* Shakespeare.

If your fiancé lusts for personalized vows but this type of artistry isn't in your locker, don't freak out. Sometimes deep emotions are tough to articulate. That's normal. *You're* normal. Thankfully, you can hire a freelance writer to transform your heartfelt word vomit into memorable vows.

After learning about you through pointed conversations or a questionnaire, this wordsmith will spill your heart with personalized eloquence. The best part? If you want to keep it a secret, no one needs to know. Search online for some variant of "wedding vow writer." I'm also a big proponent of freelance marketplaces such as Fiverr (fiverr.com) and Upwork (upwork.com). As always, check the reviews before you book.

PHOTOGRAPHY AND PAPARAZZI (PART II, FINALLY)

Before you give me lip for how long you had to read before the photography sequel, remember that sometimes the best things in life take time. At least that's how I justified waiting 10 years to propose to Jen. In the end, our marriage was the best thing that ever happened to ~~her~~ us. Just like back then, part II is worth the wait.

Your photography will dictate the bulk of your wedding-day schedule.

Remember when we discussed the magnitude of selecting a photographer with whom you get along? You're about to see why.

Yes, Grandma is a celebrity tonight.

Since your photographer will be fixating on VIPs throughout the bash, you'll need to point out these celebrities early on. Sure, you can scribble them on a piece of paper, but it's another thing entirely for your photographer to match names to faces. This is a simple fix. Recruit a couple of ambassadors from your wedding party and introduce them to your photographer before the pictures snap. Instead of your photographer peppering you with questions to learn who's who, these well-connected folks will answer on your behalf. Just make sure you enlist the social butterflies who, between them, know most attendees.

It's also a smart idea for your allies to notify your photographer of any guests who should *not* be in the camera's flash too often. Think exes and your uncle's annoying girlfriend who barely earned an invite. Taking the ambassador approach means fewer responsibilities (re: stress) for you.

TO LOOK OR NOT TO LOOK

The primary question is whether you will engage in a "first look." For the uninformed, a first look is aptly named; it's a chance for the groom to see the bride before the ceremony. It's a dramatic affair, and your photographer will swarm you with a slew of pictures along the way. A first look gives you plenty of time to take photos before your guests arrive for the ceremony.

If you've opted for a photojournalistic approach, this is the ideal time to manage any desired formal shots—while everyone is still fresh. Make sure you have this list penned well in advance and discuss this list with your photographer because they'll be pulling the strings. Don't forget to coordinate with all those who made the cut for these shots.

Look first at your receiving line.

If you opt for a receiving line after the ceremony, I strongly recommend a photo-packed first look before the ceremony. There's simply not enough time before your reception to have a robust receiving line and then take pictures, especially if you want your guests to eat dinner at some point. Hint: you do. The only exception is for weddings with a modest guest list.

If you hope to attend a solid chunk of your cocktail hour, you're better off with a first look. The downside to a first look—especially from traditionalists—is that it dampens the drama of the groom first gazing on the bride when she's walking down the aisle. Whether this matters is a personal preference.

If you forgo a first look, you will likely spend most of cocktail hour taking pictures with your new spouse and your families. This is also when the lion's share of the formal shots occurs. It's not uncommon for newlyweds to bypass cocktail hour entirely and then make a grand entrance at the reception. Thank goodness you stuffed your face with appetizers at the tasting.

First-look considerations are worth… a look.

A blend of emotion and logistics will impact your first-look decision. While Jen and I loved the idea of me first seeing her when she walked down the aisle, it was a logistical headache because we wished to take photos outside before the sun set. Do you face a similar dilemma?

We also found the first look to be the more intimate choice because we shared the moment just between us (and our photographer) as opposed to all our guests. I learned my tear ducts do in fact work when I first saw Jen. She was enamored by it; I was relieved I did my part.

FORMAL SHOTS

Once the reception kicks off, you'll be partying your tails off to celebrate ~~the end of wedding planning~~ your marriage. As such, the opportunity for formal shots dwindles. While it's not always popular, some couples choose to take pictures with each table during dinner service to ensure everyone makes the photo reels.

Ad hoc posed photos are more common—think pictures with classmates from your alma mater or shots with extended family. If you're interested in snaps of this nature, tell your photographer early in the day; time has a strange way of speeding up during the reception, especially when alcohol is involved. You'll need your photographer to nudge your guests into these shots when you inevitably forget.

Even if you don't opt for dinner-service photos, it's still an ideal time for you to greet each of your guests. Take advantage of it. Unfortunately, it's also why half your steak will likely stay on your plate.

WEDDING-DAY TIPS

Welcome to *it*: the big day. Feelings that describe this day include excitement, anxiety, panic, fear, jubilation, jitteriness, ecstasy, and relief—like I-can't-believe-I-survived-wedding-planning relief. Whatever your noun, remember that your feelings are normal. It's okay to be freaking out a little bit. In fact, it's expected.

The morning of your wedding day might drag with anticipation, but once the afternoon hits, expect a runaway train that won't slow for days. Because your wedding experience is as unique as you are, I want to share some tips for cutting stress and savoring the incredible event that lies before you:

- **Calories are energy.** Eating is still important today. Your body will not magically start cultivating its own strength just because it's your wedding day. Don't go overboard with heavy meals, but you absolutely need to eat throughout the day. Protein bars are spot on, especially with wedding-day nerves. *Do not* be adventurous with your eating today by trying new cuisines. Stick to what your stomach knows to avoid bathroom stress later—perhaps the worst kind of stress.

- **Do what keeps you calm.** For some of us, that's socializing with out-of-town friends and family. For others, it's reading or watching TV alone. Maybe a *light* workout without the risk of tearing something. How do *you* decompress? Save an early sliver of time so you start the day in the right state of mind. Be deliberate about this when penciling in your wedding-day schedule.

- **Deputize your allies.** Ensure your wedding party's roles (and those of close friends and family) are delegated and understood. Ideally, you've discussed this before today, but there's no harm in amplifying the message on game day. Need your maid of honor to be your verbal punching bag from 10:00 a.m. onward? Remind her. Expecting your best friend to record the speeches? Explain to him that there will be speeches. Then remind him. These early-day confirmations will keep you calm later.

- **Release.** Today is not the day to hold anything in. If you identify as an introvert, try a morning journal entry to memorialize your feelings. Speak to your friends or family if you're nervous. Be gracious to the staff. Give thanks to all your guests and leave no doubt about how much you appreciate their presence. Reaffirm to your partner how much they mean to you and how lucky you feel.

- **Stick with your partner.** Take a minute to greet your college entourage and out-of-town friends but save reliving the glory days for the after-party. You'll face wave after wave of heroes who want to shower you with love and congratulatory messages; these are more meaningful when received as a couple. You'll wish to remember this time with your better half above all else.

- **Steal some alone time.** In a similar vein, try to grab a moment with your new spouse immediately following the ceremony. Seeking refuge in the bridal suite or another private enclave will do the trick. Breathe the words "husband" and/or "wife" for the first time, ogle each other's stunning appearance, admire your wedding bands, devour some cheese. You know, the *fun* stuff. To facilitate this euphoria, enlist someone early (day-of coordinator, bridal attendant, loved one, etc.) to deliver some hors d'oeuvres and drinks to your space after the ceremony. Remember, this aside may be the only precious one-on-one time you're afforded until you're back in your hotel room at night's end. Use it fully.

- **Que sera, sera (don't sweat the small stuff).** This isn't our first time discussing this proverb. Excellent memory. It's just as critical now as it was during planning, so it bears repeating. You're at the point of no return—a phenomenal spot to be. Today is about rolling with the punches and keeping the focus on you and your partner, not on the details. The universe has a mystifying way of having your back.

- **Relish.** It's a little frightening how quickly the night will whisk by. You spent countless hours painstakingly planning every what-if and then the whole shebang is over before your second trip to the bar. Consciously breathe it all in. Roam around for a few minutes during your reception just to observe and remember it all. Look around during your ceremony. Immerse yourself in the moment. I bet you can't do this without smiling.

If you're unsure where to start on your wedding day, it's quite simple. Start your day with the age-old question before you face the world: am I wearing pants? Build from there, one foot in front of the other. Just like always.

DELIVERANCE: INTO THE SUNSET

To quote Dr. Ian Malcolm from *Jurassic Park*, "You did it. You crazy son of a bitch, you did it." After your wedding, you are a freshly minted resident of cloud nine, brimming with joy and disbelief.

Don't forget to be proud of yourself—ridiculously proud. *I'm* proud of you and we haven't even met! Planning and executing your wedding is significantly more than a simple rite of passage. You're almost ready to get back to "normal" life. I assure you this life exists, and I assure you it's every bit as sweet as you dreamed it would be.

My valedictory advice is this: remember to give heartfelt thanks to all those who made your wedding possible. Besides the obvious—financial contributors and décor assemblers—recall how many of your guests took long trips, gave wildly generous gifts, and helped you celebrate an incredible milestone. These comrades deserve thanks above and beyond a thank-you card.

Sincere gratitude will prolong your bliss. It elevates the superficial "yay, we're married" to the ethereal "we're incredibly blessed." *That* is what you'll savor in the days ahead.

When the chaos ends, I hope what you learned about positive thinking and managing stress remains. These tricks aren't meant to fade away like your honeymoon tan (or sunburn) but serve as a beacon when stress returns. There's good news and bad news on this front. The good news? You're going to have plenty of opportunities to use this advice after your wedding. The bad news? Well, the same. Life is stressful, folks, but it's also beautifully rewarding. Accomplishment arises from conquering the stress—exactly like you did. Just imagine what you'll accomplish next. Congratulations.

AFTERWORD

Thank you for reading *Wedding Planning Sucks: How to Conquer the Process with Less Stress*. I hope you found it a useful springboard for your wedding-planning triumph. It's an incredible honor to be included in your journey.

I hope you enjoyed reading as much as I enjoyed writing. If you have a moment, **please tell other future wedding veterans what you liked about this book by posting a review on Amazon**. I greatly appreciate it!

Finally, please stay in touch. I can't wait to tell you how proud I am of you. Let me know how it all went at weddingplanningsucks.com and you may even get featured on the site! Remember, everyone *loves* success stories—especially yours!

Thank you again.

Until next time,

WORKS CITED

Bushman, Brad J. "Does Venting Anger Feed or Extinguish the Flame? Catharsis, Rumination, Distraction, Anger, and Aggressive Responding." *Personality and Social Psychology Bulletin* 28, no. 6 (June 2002): 724–31. Accessed 2020. http://www-personal.umich.edu/~bbushman/PSPB02.pdf

"Catharsis." APA Dictionary of Psychology. Accessed 2020. https://dictionary.apa.org/catharsis.

"Foods That Help Tame Stress." Diet for Stress Management: Carbs, Nuts, and Other Stress-Relief Foods. WebMD. Accessed 2020. https://www.webmd.com/diet/ss/slideshow-diet-for-stress-management

Gonzalez, Michael J, and Jorge R Miranda-Massari. "Diet and Stress." *The Psychiatric Clinics of North America* 37, no. 4 (2014): 579–89. Accessed 2020. https://www.academia.edu/21083281/Diet_and_Stress

Hackney, Anthony C. "Stress and the Neuroendocrine System: The Role of Exercise as a Stressor and Modifier of Stress." *Expert Review of Endocrinology & Metabolism* 1, no. 6 (2006): 783–92. Accessed 2020. https://www.ncbi.nlm.nih.gov/pmc/articles/PMC2953272

Mills, Harry, Natalie Reiss, and Mark Dombeck. "Types of Stressors (Eustress vs. Distress)." Mental Help.net: An American Addiction Centers Resource. Accessed 2020. https://www.mentalhelp.net/stress/types-of-stressors-eustress-vs-distress

Scheff, Thomas J. *Catharsis in Healing, Ritual, and Drama*. Lincoln, NE: iUniverse.com, 2001. Quoted in Esta Powell. "Catharsis in Psychology and Beyond: A Historic Overview." Accessed 2020. http://primal-page.com/cathar.htm

"Sleep, Learning, and Memory." Healthy Sleep. Harvard Medical School. Accessed 2020. http://healthysleep.med.harvard.edu/healthy/matters/benefits-of-sleep/learning-memory

"Stress and Sleep." American Psychological Association. Accessed 2020. https://www.apa.org/news/press/releases/stress/2013/sleep

"Stress and Your Health: MedlinePlus Medical Encyclopedia." MedlinePlus. U.S. National Library of Medicine. Accessed 2020. https://medlineplus.gov/ency/article/003211.htm

VandenBos, Gary R. *APA Dictionary of Psychology*. Washington, DC: American Psychological Association, 2007. Quoted in Esta Powell. "Catharsis in Psychology and Beyond: A Historic Overview." Accessed 2020. http://primal-page.com/cathar.htm.

Weir, Kirsten. "The Exercise Effect." Monitor on Psychology. American Psychological Association, December 2011. Accessed 2020. https://www.apa.org/monitor/2011/12/exercise

"Working out Boosts Brain Health." American Psychological Association. Accessed 2020. https://www.apa.org/topics/exercise-stress

INDEX

A

after party
   importance of, 124
   plan ahead, 123
   venue inclusive, 53
alcohol. *See* bars
American Psychological Association (APA), 79, 85–86

B

bands. *See* music
bank accounts
   budget estimations, 39–40
   interest, 51–52
   joint or separate, 50–51
   wedding, tracking, 60
bars
   cash bar, 124, 154–155
   open bar, 118, 124, 154
   opt for two, 111
Boston University, 85
bride
   bride is always/usually right, 25–26
budgets
   budgeting apps, 48–49
   expectations of, 46–47
   floral, cost-cutting, 136–137
   perfect budget, fairy tale of, 61
   priorities, 62–63
   save rate, calculating your, 41–42, 44–45
   snafus happen, 62
Bushman, Brad, 79

C

cake. *See* wedding cake
catering
   costs, 53
   on-site vs. off-site, 104, 115, 150
catharsis
   definition of, 79
   verbal punching bags, 80
children and babies, 113, 117, 168
civil ceremonies, 158–159
cocktail hour
   Look Before You Leap, 154
   menu/appetizers, 40, 104, 149, 152
   music, 144
   photos during, 193
   venue inclusive, 4, 24, 108
communication
   guests, with your, 155
   open and honest, with partner, 13, 16, 79, 167
   Rob's Hot Take, 15–16
   vendors, with your, 139
compromise
   partner, with your, 23, 25, 140, 168
   Rob's Hot Take, 24
   tips/insight, 24, 110, 144
costs
   band/DJ, 55. *See also* music
   breaking down the, 52
   casu marzu, 53
   contracts and, 117
   florists, 54. *See also* flowers
   miscellaneous costs, master list, 56–59
   paper/stationary, 55–56. *See also* invitations
   photography, 53. *See also* photographer
   replace estimates with actual, 50
   venue/catering, largest percentage of, 53
courthouse weddings, 107, 159

D

debt conquering
   avalanche method, 71–72
   focusing on, 72
   snowball method, 70
dinner service
   buffet option, 112, 153
   dietary restrictions, 150, 153
   menu selection, 23, 104, 152–153

tasting, 114, 151–152
vegetarians, 153
DIY (do-it-yourself)
   money saving ideas, 63, 133, 138, 179–181
DJs. *See* music
Dombeck, Mark, 68–69
dress codes, 172

E

emotions
   negativity, feelings of, 13, 70, 73–74, 81
   suppressing/expressing, 79, 191
exercise
   stress reducing, 85–86, 92

F

finances, personal, 50
first look 192–193, 194
flowers
   cost of, 41, 54, 135
   florist, selecting, 136, 138
   wedding flower substitutes, 137–138
food. *See* dinner service

G

Gonzalez, Michael J, 86
groom
   right on occasion, 26
guests
   accommodations/transportation for, 122–123
   contact information, maintaining, 166
   desire to impress, 89
   don't care, 89–91
   guest list, crafting, 167–168

H

Hackney, Anthony, 95
help
   asking for, 68, 77
   financial, 41, 43
holidays, schedule wedding during, 100
home weddings, 105–106
honeymoon
   tips and suggestions, 184–185
hospitality, 122, 163
hotels, 122

I

insurance. *See* wedding day
invitations
   B-list invitees, 170–171
   design, 171–172
   envelope printing, 166
   mail out, when to, 169
   save-the-dates, sending out, 165–166
   stamps required, 172
   tips and tricks, 173–174

L

listening, art of, 26, 35, 85, 90

M

marriage
   more than a wedding, 82, 92, 107, 166
   pre-marriage counseling, 158
marriage license, 28, 56, 172
marriage licensing made easy, 160
mashed potato bar, 90
Microsoft Excel/Google Sheets. *See* spreadsheets
Mills, Harry, 68–69
Miranda-Massari, Jorge R, 96
music
   bands, selection of, 141, 146
   ceremony/reception, 144
   cost assessment, 143
   DIY music, 146
   DJs, selecting a reputable, 142, 145–146
   must-play/do-not-play lists, 145–147

N

name change, 50
negativity
   accepting, 73–74
negotiating. *See* venue

O

officiant
   selection of, 157
Otto, Michael, 84–85

P

panic, feelings of, 28, 68, 194
photographer/videographer
   contracts/questions to ask, 134–135
   cost of, 53–54
   invest a little extra, 128, 134
   relationship with, 128, 131, 133
   selection of, 127–128, 131
photography
   digital vs. film, 132
   formal shots, 192–194
   instant camera, 180–181
   mixed styles, 129–130

photo booths, 133, 180–181
photojournalistic style/candid shots, 129
posed photos, 130, 194
rights, 133
traditional style photography, 128
Pinterest, 130, 136, 156
plus plus
    administrative fee/sales tax, 117–118, 120
prioritize, 35, 93–94
productivity
    increasing your, 14, 69–70, 78, 84

Q

questions to ask
    at-home venues, 105–106
    caterer, off site, 150–151
    DJ/band, 144, 148–149
    florist, 139–140
    officiant, the, 161
    photographer, 132, 134–135
    venue/staff, 112–116

R

Ramsey, Dave, 71
receiving line, 193
reception
    costs of, 53
    decorating/decorations, 136–137
    different day than wedding, 107
    finding the perfect, 102
    music, 143–144, 146–147
    open bar vs. cash bar, 154–155
    red flags, 102, 110
    transportation to/from, 108
registry
    do's and don'ts, 174–175
    practical tips, 175–176
rehearsal dinner, 59, 79, 113, 123
Reiss, Natalie, 68–69
religious concerns
    clergy, selection of. *See* officiant
    house of worship, 107–108, 138, 157
RSVP cards, 170, 173

S

same team, stay on the, 14, 63, 75–75, 167
schadenfreude, 87
Scheff, Thomas, 79
Selye, Hans, 68
Smits, Jasper, 85
spreadsheet
    categories, 56–59

free download available (weddingplanningsucks.com), 31
Rob's Hot Take, 176
setting up your, 29–30
staying organized, 31–32
tracking progress, 30–31
variables, sample of, 45
stress. *See also* catharsis; exercise; same team
    accepting negativity, 73
    ask for help, 77–78
    distress, effects of, 69
    eustress, good stress, 69–70
    financial. *See* debt conquering
    journaling your thoughts, 81–82
    physical/emotional tension, defined as, 68
    professional help, when to seek, 68
    reduce with positive thinking, 74
    reduction, cheat sheet, 91–92
    remember the why, 82
    set priorities, 83–84, 89
    shut out the noise, 76–77
    sleep issues and, 85–86
    unhealthy to healthy eating patterns, 86–87

T

tactical fun, 84
tactical silence, 26–27
tipping, 118, 141
title changes, 83
to-do lists
    add to spreadsheet, 29–30
    creating as you go, 28
    tackling, 70–71, 77, 92
    tracking, 31
transportation considerations, 123

V

vegetarians. *See* dinner service
venue
    all-in-one considerations, 4, 23–24
    at-home option, 105–106
    budget, 53–55
    contract, 33, 62, 104
    fine print, 118–119
    negotiations, 119–120
    perks, ask for additional, 121
    walkthroughs, 109–110
vows. *See* wedding vows

W

WebMD, 86
wedding budget, 6, 52
wedding cake, 155–156
wedding day
    bridal party dressing rooms, 122–123
    insurance, at-home venue 106
    missteps/blunders, 87–88
    tips, 43, 194–195
wedding dress/tuxedo, 55–56
wedding planner
    day of coordinator, 33
    month of planner, 34
    professional, costs of, 34–35
    read the reviews, 35
    traditional, 32
wedding planning
    life experience, as a, 1–2, 14, 18
    negativity, challenges of, 73–74
    perspective on, 89
    Rob's Hot Take, 26–27, 84
    staying positive, 72–73
    weddingplanningsucks.com, 31, 118, 149
wedding season, 99–100
wedding vows
    ask for help/advice, 191
    self-written vows, 189–190
    traditional/conventional vows, 189
wedding websites, 167
welcome bags, 55, 59, 184
welcome drinks, 59, 123

Made in the USA
Middletown, DE
29 September 2023

39737593R00126